THE

Fundamentals

OF

BUSINESS
-TO-
BUSINESS

Sales and Marketing

THE

Fundamentals

OF

BUSINESS -TO- BUSINESS

Sales and Marketing

JOHN M. COE

McGraw-Hill

New York   Chicago   San Francisco   Lisbon   London   Madrid   Mexico City
Milan   New Delhi   San Juan   Seoul   Singapore   Sydney   Toronto

The *McGraw·Hill* Companies

Library of Congress Cataloging-in-Publication Data

Coe, John M.
    The fundamentals of business-to-business sales and marketing / John M. Coe.
        p.   cm.
    Includes index.
    ISBN 0-07-140879-7
    1. Selling.   2. Industrial marketing.   3. Selling—Data processing.   4. Sales
management.   I. Title.

    HF5438.25.C64   2003
    658.8'04—dc21   2003000689

10 11 12 13 14 15 16 IBT/IBT 1 9 8 7 6 5 4 3 2

ISBN-13: 978-0-07-140879-0

ISBN-10: 0-07-140879-7

McGraw-Hill books are available at special quantity discounts to use as premiums and sales promotions, or for use in corporate training programs. For more information, please write to the Director of Special Sales, Professional Publishing, McGraw-Hill, Two Penn Plaza, New York, NY 10121-2298. Or contact your local bookstore.

This book is printed on acid-free paper.

To my wife, Cheri, who always understood when I went to my "cave" to write this book—I love you!

To my daughter, Michelle, who avoided my thoughts for her to follow in my footsteps and went on to greater achievements as a Christian, teacher, wife, and mother of two wonderful children,
Jessica and Megan

To Al Hogan, my "little brother," who went from being mentored about life to mentoring me in all matters technical, and growing up to make any parent proud

Contents

Preface

How DID I get here? A Harvard study decades ago tracked college graduates to see how many stayed in their area of study. My memory is that only about 35 percent did. I'm certainly part of the other 65 percent. Not only did I not stay with my college major, chemistry, but I also left my first career in sales to become what—a direct marketer?

Funny thing, most of my colleagues have the same story of meandering career paths. Nobody really started out with the goal of a career in direct marketing. So what was the turning point for me?

It happened back in 1979 when I was VP of Sales and Marketing for a company in Chicago. I reported to the president, who had a background in manufacturing and finance, and who was also a screamer—have you ever worked for a screamer? No fun, I can assure you. One fall day he entered my office and began to unload on me, in no uncertain terms, that my department represented 13.5 percent of the total revenue of the company. As he reached the climax of his visit, his voice was in the high decibel range and his face was turning red. I guess this was the first time he had calculated this, and even though I had been on the job for less than a year, he blamed me for this apparent great waste of money. Secretly, I knew he didn't really like sales guys anyway and the money we spent on silly things like customer entertaining.

As he finished and was almost out the door, he turned and shouted out my key goal for the upcoming fiscal year—"Bring that down to 12.5

percent and, of course, your sales goal stays the same." Silence at last but my head was swimming—how in the hell could I meet the revenue objective with what amounted to an eight percent cut in the budget? If I cut money it would mean cutting some of our 110 salespeople, as we didn't really spend that much money on marketing. On the other hand, we had already looked at the sales coverage and were putting in place a new sales organization and coverage model to improve call rates and sales efficiency.

The only answer was to do something I didn't know how to do—increase overall marketing and sales productivity. Fortunately for me, I was in Chicago and had heard of a group called the Chicago Association of Direct Marketing. I had recently gotten an announcement of a meeting featuring Shell Alpert, a well-known consultant who was speaking on business direct marketing. That sounded good even though I didn't even know what that meant. I went, listened, and it changed my life. In fact, I stumbled over direct marketing.

As a result, we quickly instituted a direct mail and modest telemarketing program that focused on removing the need for sales to make cold calls. That small change freed up enough time for them to call on customers with higher sales opportunities. And guess what—it worked. We met the challenge and at the end of the year had reduced the 13.5 percent to 12.0 percent and met the revenue goal. Along the way, I screamed back one day and he stopped screaming at me—don't know if it was because I screamed back or because we met the sales goal.

As they say, the rest is history, and I'm now writing a book about something I stumbled across almost twenty-five years ago. Do things come full circle or what? In those twenty-five years, B2B sales and marketing methods have seen some changes (who would have thought of the Internet in 1979?), but there are still far too many things that have stayed the same.

For almost all the clients I have worked with and all the ones I hear about, improving sales and marketing productivity is clearly job number one. No longer can we continue with the old methods, as they just aren't working and are too costly. That is obvious to all. The bigger issue is what to do and how to do it? This is what the book is all about, and for me it started twenty-five years ago. During the intervening years, I learned a lot and have many experiences to share—many of them are in this book.

Frankly, I'm excited about what lies ahead for B2B sales and marketing. I've again changed careers and now want to spread the word, and therefore have started the Sales and Marketing Institute, a consulting, education, and training firm. I'll end my career odyssey spreading the word on how to achieve the dichotomous goals of "sell more" and "spend less." I guess the screamer had a point!

THE

Fundamentals

OF

BUSINESS -TO- BUSINESS

Sales and Marketing

1

Why Is It So Tough
to Sell Today?

THE FIRST THING you must know before reading this book is where I'm coming from—or in more finely tuned words, what's my perspective? Simply, I'm a salesman! I started my career in the chemical and plastic industry as a sales trainee at B.F. Goodrich Chemical in Cleveland, after graduating from Miami University of Ohio with a chemistry degree (another way to say I dropped out of premed). After a year of sales and product training, I found myself in product management, but I eventually returned to my salesman goal and joined the Chemical Division of Quaker Oats as a technical representative covering five states. After several years of selling and a promotion to district manager, along with several more years of road warriorship, I landed my first big break—the position of national sales manager.

Being sales manager at Quaker Oats Chemical was really a dual job. The first was managing the sales group, which, by the way, included three district managers who were over age fifty and not very happy to be managed by a thirty-year-old long-haired guy (remember the '70s). The second responsibility was to act as the national account manager for our large customers, which included a long list of Fortune 500 companies.

Several other positions followed in the next several years with smaller firms, as director of sales and marketing and finally vice president of sales and marketing. All along the way, I spent most of my time in the field with our salespeople and customers; I really was a sales guy even though my title changed.

Sales Experience Matters

In essence, my first fifteen years in business were spent directly in selling or heavily sales-oriented positions. Why am I telling you this? Not to impress you but to clearly establish my point of view—that of a salesperson. Most of the books, articles, seminars, and conferences on the subject approach the functions of marketing and sales from the broader viewpoint of marketing. Yes, in the classic marketing definition (sometimes called marketing with a capital *M*) sales is a part of marketing. In the real world, the sales group almost always dominates marketing within a company and is the power source between the two.

A quick definition of marketing is required at this point. Marketing involves three groups: product/market management, marketing communications, and sales. At times, customer service is included in the "big M" definition as well. Typically, product management exists to manage the product development, pricing, technical support, and so on, of the products and/or services the company offers to the market. My references to marketing in this book relate to the marketing communication function and not the product management role. The two must integrate closely for the company to be successful, but the issues facing product management are quite different and generally do not deal directly with the development of marketing communications targeted at prospects and customers. In fact, at IBM the product groups were called "sponsors," as they had the responsibility of the group's profit and loss and therefore the budget. We in marketing communications had to present plans and programs to these "sponsors" to obtain our budget dollars. In some companies, the product managers think they know how to do everything and try to also play the role of the marketing communications department—usually with poor results.

In fact, until the early 1990s the marketing communications group was typically relegated to developing sales literature, creating and placing advertising in trade journals, arranging for trade shows, and other such activities. The responsibility to drive revenue and profit clearly resided with the sales organization. Yet, I hear intelligent marketing communications individuals pontificating on how the sales group needs to change. With few exceptions, these same individuals have never really held a field sales position. Yes, they do sell concepts and ideas internally, but they have no real in-the-field experience.

What's a field sales experience like? Well, it's planning out your week of calls; phoning for appointments; driving or flying to the account locations; waiting in lobbies; seeing customers and potential ones; following up on items requested; writing trip reports and recording in your "sales book" information that you need to remember. Today the sales book may be ACT on the laptop, but you'll read more about sales force automation (a horrible term) later in the book. Then, once this week is over, it's doing it again and again—not quite like the movie *Groundhog Day* but close. It's a grind, to be sure, but real salespeople wouldn't have it any other way, as there are many benefits to offset the grind. The ones that I valued the most were the adrenaline rush of closing the deal, the independence and ability to take action now, plus all the personal relationships and fun to be had along the way. For anyone who is planning a marketing communication campaign that involves the sales staff, understanding this "road warrior" life is mandatory to launching requests and designing feedback systems that are directed at field salespeople. The old phrase "You need to walk a mile in my shoes" has an important and double meaning when it comes to understanding and working with salespeople.

I could go on, but I think I've made the point. So, why is this important? Well, frankly, the days when sales ruled and delivered results are over. The sales group now needs help, and this book is all about deploying a new sales model that fundamentally alters the "go-to-market" sales and marketing strategy. This new sales model integrates the functions of marketing communications and sales in a way not visualized by anyone before the 1990s. Up until now, much of the academic dialogue dealt with this "integration" from the viewpoint of the marketing department in the home office. How do you think customer relationship management, or the now-infamous CRM, was received by sales? Not well, I can assure you. In B2B this home-office approach to improving the company's sales revenue is just wrong. To do it right, we need to start from the perspective of the salesperson. There are millions of salespeople in the United States, as counted by *Sales and Marketing Management* magazine. They carry great responsibility and still manage the primary customer relationship. Any new system that doesn't start from this viewpoint in B2B is doomed to fail as somewhere between 55 and 70 percent of CRM implementations have failed. (The Gartner Group reports 55 percent and The Butler Group reports 70 percent failure.)

Several years ago, I was giving a presentation on the appeal and power of direct marketing as the technique for companies to retool their sales coverage models. Someone from the audience said, "John, you got it all wrong. Sales shouldn't integrate with direct marketing; marketing needs to integrate with sales." I'm only sorry that I can't give the individual credit here, as I didn't get his name, but thanks—you're right!

So, why is it so much harder to sell today? Well, the old model of how B2B companies went to market is breaking down. The following sections explore four major trends causing the breakdown.

Customers Don't Want to See Salespeople Anymore

Let's clarify the foregoing statement, as there are still 11.9 million salespeople in the United States, and I am not implying that they should all be out of work. A more accurate perspective is that customers don't want to see salespeople when either they feel they don't need to or don't believe it will help them in their buying process. That said, when an important negotiation is required, or a key problem or question arises, a sales contact often is not only desired but sought by the customer. This trend is a far cry from the '70s and '80s, when customers relied primarily on the salesperson for information and guidance regarding products and services coupled with the comfort brought by a personal relationship. In conversations these days with companies, both large and small, I almost always hear someone remark, "Our salespeople can't get to the key buyers anymore." What's happened?

The Value of a Salesperson to Buyers

Andersen Consulting (now Accenture) used to survey industrial buyers (not just purchasing people) on the characteristics they most valued in their suppliers. In 1970 the results of this survey showed that the most important characteristic buyers valued in companies they did business with was "a knowledgeable and capable outside salesperson." Other vendor and/or product attributes that followed in importance included price, service, and quality. The survey was repeated every ten years, and by 1990 the value of the sales call had fallen to eighth place! In 1990 first place was "the availability of a capable *inside* salesperson." Quite a comedown for the field sales group. Unfortunately, Accenture did not repeat this survey in 2000, so the results are not current. Nevertheless, for at least twelve years the market had been saying, "We really don't want to see salespeople," and that was before the advent of the Internet and E-business. Frankly, until recently, most sales organizations haven't been listening to their prospects and customers on this point. Why do you think salespeople are still told to go sit in the lobbies of potential or current customers?

The field salesperson has been gradually seeing this lack of receptiveness. Here's an example. In 1994 I was asked to help out a friend of one of my best friends, Bill Kassner. Bill's friend was having a hard time reentering the office supply business in Cincinnati after a ten-year absence. Here's what he had to say: "In 1984, the year I left the office supply business, I could go down the street and make ten calls and see eight office managers. But today if I make the same ten calls, I can only see one or two. What happened?" Well, what happened is catalogs, superstores, and inbound call centers. (This was all before the Internet.) In this industry category, the field salesperson had become "not needed" by the office managers. Other sources of information and buying options were now available. This made seeing a salesperson more of a waste of time, as it added no value to the buyer or the transaction. I would imagine that if an office supply salesperson made a call now on these companies, he or she might be met with shock by the office manager. On the other hand, at large companies where contracts are negotiated and complex servicing is required, a salesperson still has value. In most cases, an inside salesperson is the primary human contact in the office supply business (combined with frequent direct mailing, catalogs, and E-mails).

Time Is the Saleperson's Enemy

This issue of time or, I should say, the lack thereof, has also made the salesperson's job more difficult. Today no businesspeople feel they have enough time to do their jobs, and when they're asked by a salesperson for an appointment, this "lack of time" causes most of them to defer the request. In other words, less time on the part of buyers translates to resistance to see salespeople. This resistance is also based on the "Why do we need to meet?" question heard so often today. "Can we handle this on the phone?" "Does your website contain the information you want to tell me?" "Do you have an inside person I can call when I have questions?" These expressions of resistance combined with the time shortage really make it tough today for salespeople to persuade buyers to see them on a regular basis.

Buyers now are far more educated about and comfortable with non–face-to-face and virtual communications to evaluate product or service solutions before making the buying decision. In fact, several years ago I interviewed an engineer regarding how he made specification decisions on equipment he was designing. Here's what he said: "I only do business with companies who have a website containing all the technical information on their products plus an inside technical sales representative who can answer my questions when I call. I cannot wait for a salesperson to call me back or visit as by that time I've had to make my decision, since our design time cycles are so short today."

Three Calls per Day Is Now the Norm

Up until recently, all the surveys done on how many sales calls a salesperson made in a day showed that the average was four. For smaller local sales territories, the number was higher, and for extended drive/fly territories, of course, it was lower. As a sales manager, I always calculated the maximum number of sales calls for each salesperson by using 200 to 220 selling days per year multiplied by four calls per day, for a total of between 800 and 880 calls per year per salesperson. This gave me a baseline on how best to organize territory loads between salespeople, since if there were too many customers to call on, we would logically not cover the territory properly and lose sales. In 2001 *Sales and Marketing Management* released a study that showed that this decades-old average of four had shrunk to three—a whopping 25 percent reduction in sales productivity! I recently visited a large company with 800 salespeople where the calls per day had decreased to 1.5 from 3.5 in just the last five years. Of course, the national average and this company's call rate didn't drop in one year but rather was declining over time, all due to the previously mentioned issues.

Communication Clutter Is High and Getting Worse

Advertising messages are now coming at us from new and multiple sources: in restaurant rest rooms (on the backs of stalls and now actually on the toilet paper), on panels in airport baggage claim belts, on the sides of cars and buses, in pop-ups on websites, and so on, and so on. Here are some scary statistics:

• *Advertising Age* reported in 2000 that the average number of messages we either see or hear daily is now between 4,000 and 5,000.

• This followed a 1999 Intertec report documenting that messages directed at us had increased sixfold in the last twenty years to 3,000 per day.

• A 2000 Pitney Bowes study found that in the office we receive 204 messages a day in the United States. Other countries are not far behind: 191 in the United Kingdom, 178 in Germany, and 165 in France.

• In 2001 an estimated 1.4 trillion E-mail messages were sent by businesses—up from 40 billion in 1995. On top of that, in early 2003 nearly 40 percent of all E-mail messages sent were spam, and by the end of the year, industry experts expect that number to reach 50 percent. Talk about clutter! How many E-mails do you now get each day at home and at the office?

This message (pun intended) is clear: we have become an overcommunicated society, and most of us have reached a point of "sensory overload." We are just tuning out messages both wanted and unwanted. Studies have shown that we now delete more than 70 percent of E-mail messages when we don't instantly recognize the sender, and who could blame us? Here's a test: try to remember more than one or two messages you received yesterday. Better yet, did you respond to any of them? Our problem is clear—for both sales and marketing people: how are we going to break through the clutter and be heard by our current and potential customers? To sell, you first have to be heard, and the traditional role of marketing communications was to try to loudly announce to the potential buyers the reason they should see the salesperson. Now it's difficult to even get to the ear of the buyer, let alone to actually be heard.

Awareness Does Not Equal Behavior Anymore

Even if the buyer has heard the marketing communications and is aware of the company and the brand, there is another problem to face. Awareness does not drive behavior anymore. Behavior, or what people do, is driven more by offers and deals than just awareness. I will not debate the value of a positive brand image or high product awareness in the mind of the buyer; they are both important. But how much will it cost to achieve such goals in view of all the clutter we must fight through? Even if we create a high awareness of the product or service within the targeted market(s), business buying decisions are based on more significant parameters. In the past, salespeople broke through the clutter using the impact of a personal sales call. So, the question is, how do we now break through the clutter and communicate to the decision makers and influencers if the buyers can't hear our message and don't want to see salespeople?

The Buying Process Is More Complex

Long gone are the days when one person made the company's buying decisions. That may still be the procedure for known commodities, like office supplies, sold to smaller companies in which one person (generally the owner) does the buying. Beyond that simple situation, the buying process becomes increasingly complex. Here's an example. Years ago, the computer companies, such as IBM and Apple, focused on the information technology manager to purchase technology. Today technology companies will tell you that in addition to the IT group, you must also satisfy the application users, finance, purchasing, and even upper management. This more complex purchasing scenario is repeated in other industries as well. Teaming or matrix management has also increased the complexity of the buying/sales process. This is particularly true when the product or service being bought is of high importance or carries a high price. In larger companies the team members who are charged with the buying decision may not even be in the same location or city, which adds another complication for the sales group. Recently I talked to a bright marketing communications manager who had identified three types of individuals in his targeted high-tech market to whom he needed to communicate:

- One economic buyer (typically the CFO)
- Two user buyers (several groups of users typically existed)
- Two IT buyers (the department head and the application support engineer)

The problem he faced was to find the names of these five individuals, as no list contained a complete record of all the names in each company needed for his direct mail program. This example highlights the issue; there are many more people to find and contact than in the "old" days when one or two people made a purchasing decision.

The Buying Process Versus the Sales Cycle

In days past, the salesperson was in direct contact with the buyer or buyers, and the experienced salesperson would instinctively match his or her sales approach with the buyer's needs, process, and even personality. Two changes have made the selling challenge more difficult. First, the salesperson doesn't have the same level of contact with all the decision makers and influencers. Second, the buying process has been extended and made more complex with the addition of more functions and people. Following is an example of steps in a typical sales cycle versus the buying process. The product in this example is of critical importance to the buyer and carries a high price, both of which add steps and lengthen the buying process time line.

Sales Cycle	Buying Process
Inquiry generation	Need awareness and definition
Lead qualification	Vendor identification
Proposal/quote	Information gathering
First sale	Vendor evaluation/initial selection
Repeat sale	Request for proposal (RFP) or quote (RFQ)
	Narrowing of vendor's choices
	Demonstration/presentation by vendor(s)
	Reference checking
	Vendor selection
	Negotiation
	First purchase
	Evaluation
	Second purchase

The example yields three relevant observations:

- There are more steps in the buying process than the sales cycle.
- Sales departments continue to attempt to reduce the sales cycle time, while buyers are on a different schedule.
- The language we use to define the sales cycle and buying process are quite different from each other.

We are seeing a growing disconnect between the sales cycle and the buying process. This disconnect reduces sales results due to two separate but related actions. First, the salesperson tries to speed up or compress the sales cycle. If not successful, the salesperson will typically go on to other leads or customers from which near-term revenue is more likely to be obtained. In essence, the salesperson leaves the buyer behind even though the buyer will purchase but, of course, not from the salesperson's company. Second, a buyer who feels uncomfortable with the rushing of the sales process will retreat. Have you ever had a company force its sales process on you? If you have, then my guess is that you closed down or walked away from that company and bought elsewhere. To improve sales effectiveness, we must more closely align the sales process to the buying process of the target audience. Here it is important to note that not all segments of your market have the same buying process and therefore adjustments may well have to be made between each market segment. As an example, think of how the buying and sales process would vary if you were selling office equipment to small, medium, and large companies. For the small company, the president or owner would make the decision and it would be quick. For medium-sized firms, the office manager would likely be the decision maker and the decision would be a bit slower, but not much more complex. Now, think of a large company, such as General Motors. There would be a purchasing agent in charge of office equipment and the buying process would include a trial or demo, plus contract negotiation. I think you would agree that each decision process and person is quite different from the others. Yet I have seen companies who sell office equipment send the same mailing and offer to all three companies without any differentiation—clearly a failure in matching the sales and buying process. In addition, no rethinking of which individual should receive the mailing is done. In this case, a title slug along the lines of "Office Manager" or "Office Equipment Buyer" is stuck on the mailing label. It's not hard to see why direct response rates and lead conversion rates have declined in recent years.

I have a great example of how this "closing down" on the part of the buyer happens. Though it occurred in the consumer arena, I think we all can relate. My son-in-law, Joe Guinter, was visiting me in Scottsdale for the first time and realized that there was no rust on used cars in Arizona. He and my daughter Michelle live in the community of Bay Village outside Cleveland, where they both grew up, and have spent their whole lives in snow and salt—a recipe for rust. They needed a good used car, and Joe thought that buying one in Arizona would be a smart move. We went car shopping one Saturday and visited several used car lots attached to new car dealers. At the second one, a salesperson spied us and introduced himself to me—the older guy. I quickly explained that it was Joe, and not me, he should be addressing. A little disappointment registered, and he then suggested to Joe that the two of them go inside before looking at any cars. A somewhat unusual request, I thought, but being a good father-in-law, I stayed back and browsed the used car lot with my daughter. In just a few minutes, Joe came bursting through the door, and as he rushed past us, he said in no uncertain terms, "We're out of here!" It was clear that Joe was finished with his buying process, and only later did I hear the story. This car salesman sat Joe down and began to qualify him as to his income and credit—all before Joe had even expressed interest in any car. This was not in keeping with his buying process; it made him upset, and he disconnected. The big mistake the salesperson made was not understanding the buyer's process and instead imposing his sales process. Obviously, he didn't sell a car to Joe and Michelle that day.

As a result of the issues discussed here, the number of sales contacts (both inside and outside sales calls) required to close a complex sale, such as the one just referenced, has risen to an average of eight or more. This compares with five in the late 1980s as documented in a McGraw-Hill study on sales call cost and productivity. The increased number of contacts required to close represents a true double whammy: more calls required to close a sale combined with fewer calls made per day! No wonder sales and marketing costs, expressed as a percentage of company revenue, have climbed dramatically in the last ten to twenty years. It's not abnormal to see total sales and marketing costs reach 15 percent to 25 percent of total company revenue. Any improvement in this measure of productivity will drop right to the bottom line.

At IBM in the early 1990s, when many people felt that this legend of American business was going out of business, the sales and general administrative (S&GA) percentage was in the mid-30s. When Lou Gerstner, the new president, arrived, he quickly recognized that sales costs had gotten way out of line. In response, he dramatically reduced the number of salespeople while, at the same time, increasing the usage of direct marketing to contact potential and current customers. There's much more to this cost reduction story, but at the end of the 1990s the S&GA percentage had fallen to the midteens, or in round numbers, a drop of 15 percent. IBM's revenue was approximately $80 billion at that point, which calculated to savings of $12 billion. In the words of the famous senator from Illinois, Everett Dirksen, "a billion here and a billion there and pretty soon you have some real money." Of course, he was talking about the federal budget, but that's the kind of impact that's possible if you can develop a new sales coverage model to attack the productivity issue.

Multiple Channels and Choices Are More Available

The buyer today has much greater selection than ever before. Not only can the buyer choose from different channels (direct, catalog, websites, distributors, et cetera), but the range of competitive solutions has increased as well.

Multiple Channels of Distribution

One of the internal debates sellers are having today is how they should "go to market." What channel(s) should they set up to offer their products and services? While this debate is a subject for a more in-depth discussion, it can be reduced to the following four key questions:

- How does the buyer want to buy?
- What are the most "customer-friendly" channels for our products or services?
- Will we lose control of the customer relationship by adding distribution channels? If so, will that eventually lead to lost sales?
- Are there sales efficiencies and cost savings or additional expense that will result from expanding the channels of distribution?

The answers to these and other questions will determine if companies will provide expanded access to their product or service offerings. In each case, the distribution choice will then open up a series of marketing needs and issues as the company realizes that working through distributors, value-added resellers (VARs), business partners, and so forth, is not the panacea that it might have appeared to be. The decrease in contact with prospects and customers combined with the lack of feedback from the channel partners creates a whole new set of sales and marketing challenges. In fact, this very lack of feedback and subsequent reduction of customer knowledge flies in the face of newer methods such as database marketing and customer relationship management. A tough choice with ramifications!

A classic example of this problem occurred at Texas Instruments in the mid-1990s. Their consultant, McKinsey, recommended that they discontinue sales coverage of small accounts and turn them over to five large national distributors. In the 1990s this was a popular move; many companies were trying to reduce sales costs and this was an obvious reduction cost. Only after this was done did it become clear to TI that while sales cost reduction had been achieved, they had effectively lost contact with these smaller customers, as these large distributors were not providing the needed feedback. These distributors competed with each other and were loath to provide TI with more than just the required minimum sales data. The distributors felt, with some justification, that these were *their* customers, so why should they tell TI anything more than required? As a result, individual contact information within TI did not exist, as until then, no customer database had been developed. To offset this lack of contact, TI initiated a database development project to generate the information that was lost when the sales group dropped coverage. The database then supported a direct mail and an outbound telemarketing effort to attempt to replace the capability to directly communicate to their customers and introduce new chip products to them. I'm not sure, in the long run, if TI actually saved money and/or grew sales to this segment.

Competition Has Many Faces Today

It used to be that competition was defined as only those companies that sold the same product or service you did. Boy, have times changed! Competition is defined today in one of three categories. Here's a brief description of each.

• **Direct:** the standard definition of companies that sell basically the same product or service. While there may be some differences in offerings, the buying decision in direct competitive situations frequently falls to price war.

• **Indirect:** companies selling different products or services that can offer the buyer the same result. An example is fax versus overnight mail. Remember when FedEx tried to open fax centers, only to have them fail? In this environment, your price may be better than that of your direct competition, but the sale may still be lost to an indirect competitor.

• **Technology:** a technology solution that provides the same result but does it in a completely different format. There are many examples. Ask yourself where the typesetters are today after the advent of sophisticated direct-to-plate printing technology. Sometimes sellers don't even realize they have lost, as buyers don't define the decision in normal competitive terms.

Defining the competitive matrix must include these two newer forms of competition and further complicates the selling job. This competitive environment has become richer for the buyer and tougher for the sales group. I've encountered many marketers who tend to dismiss or even ignore the forms of competition that are not clearly defined. By doing so, the marketers fail to address these competitors with added value or benefits that assist the sales groups in battling indirect or technology competition. In days past a salesperson had more defined competition and could present effective pitches. Now the salesperson may not even be aware of the competitive forces and therefore can't effectively fight for the order. Finally, another form of competition that frequently causes sales resistance is the "status quo" attitude on the part of the buyer. More often than salespeople care to admit, they haven't made a compelling case for the buyer to change the product or business method currently in use. Frequently, this is the hardest form of competition to overcome.

Summary

Why is it so tough to sell today? You may face a few other issues in your specific industry and market segment, but let's recount the main factors that are dramatically decreasing sales productivity today:

- Customers don't want to see salespeople and are obtaining the required information via other methods.
- Sales call rates have fallen to an average of three calls a day from four.
- Communication clutter is high and increasing; we all are on sensory overload.
- Awareness does not drive behavior anymore.
- The sales cycle is more frequently disconnected from the buying process.
- There are many more decision makers and influencers to sell.
- There are more channels that offer solutions to the buyer.
- Customer knowledge and feedback is reduced when more channels of distribution are added to the "go-to-market" model.
- The faces of competition have multiplied and now include alternate solutions that require stronger value propositions to compete.

Notice that I haven't even mentioned the cost of the sales call, which by all accounts now averages $300 to $400. Cahners recently released a report that pegs the cost per call at $329. That may be the average, but I recently had a client tell me that the company's sales call cost was $2,100! We will explore how to calculate your cost per call in later chapters, but suffice to say it is a key statistic to know.

There's Hope

Yes, it's more difficult to sell today using the traditional salesperson-based go-to-market models. That's the bad news. The good news is that a new integration between sales and marketing is emerging that is producing a new sales coverage model. The goal of this book is to fully detail this model. As a preview, here are a few of the characteristics of the new sales coverage model:

• Inquiry generation, lead qualification, and sales opportunity development are now legitimate jobs for the marketing communications department to tackle. The days when all the raw inquiries were turned over to sales are gone for good.

• Technology, in the form of software, the Internet, wireless communications, videoconferencing, web seminars, and the like, is coming to the aid of the sales and marketing group to dramatically increase the tools available for sales productivity improvements.

• Databases of prospect and customer information are being gathered and used for direct communication to prospects and customers that supplement or even supplant the salesperson's responsibility.

• Inside sales and telemarketing have grown as a method of contact that can nurture leads and sell customers in combination with face-to-face contact.

• Need we expound on the Internet and all the functionality it brings? What's exciting is that we are continuing to learn how to use this technology to assist and even create new methods of selling.

The role of the salesperson has changed, but salespeople will never go away. The salesperson still is and will remain king of the "golden moment." It's just that other people and communication methods will now be part of the sales process. No longer will the salesperson have sole responsibility for the customers. It will now be the job of both marketing communications and the sales group working together, sharing a common database of information that will be the new sales coverage model.

2

The New Sales Coverage Model

IT'S TOUGH TO SELL TODAY! No one disagrees with this. The issue is—
what to do about it?

As a former sales manager, I can report that, traditionally, the secrets
to sales success were all wrapped up in the salespeople and their effectiveness. The leverages to ensure sales success were simple:

- Hire the best salespeople you could find.
- Train, both professionally and technically, and then reinforce the
  training.
- Motivate the sales group through compensation programs and
  recognition.
- Organize sales territories fairly.
- Stand back and let people do the job, but coach like hell.
- Fire them quickly if they didn't cut it.

This list, of course, assumes that the product or service that the company was selling met a market need and was fairly priced. If that was true,
then sales success was all about the salespeople and how they performed
in the field. This environment gave me a feeling of power and control
within the company, an experience that was common then among many

other sales managers as well. Being a salesperson or a sales manager was a great job and a great life. Not anymore!

The Main Message of This Book

While there still are many salespeople, the "sales life" I lived back in the '70s and '80s is a thing of the past, and I'm not even talking about the current hassle factor in traveling. But, for companies, the real problem is that the keys to success no longer rest solely with the salespeople and sales management. These keys are now shared between the sales group and the marketing communications people. To turn the "lock," a new sales coverage model is required that mixes other forms of communication along with sales calls to form a more productive combination that achieves the dichotomous goals of "sell more" and "spend less." This is the challenge today and is what this book is all about. Quite simply, the new sales coverage model is the blending of face-to-face sales calls with other highly targeted communications throughout every phase of the customer life cycle to achieve a more productive marketing and sales result. That's the issue, and like most tough problems in business, there is no easy or fast solution. The remainder of the book is devoted to defining this new model and laying out how it can be developed and executed for your company.

What This Book Is Not About

Marketing, with a capital *M*, is a very broad subject and includes many traditional areas such as market research, product management, pricing, competitive analysis, and customer service. This book is not about those areas. Yes, they are important, but I'll leave each of those subjects to other experts. This book is also not about the creative aspects of developing advertising, direct mail packages, telemarketing scripts, or even Web pages. The creative practitioners and direct marketing agencies have lots of knowledge about creating these communications, and you should hire them to do the job. It's also not a book on technology, even though software applications for sales and marketing are growing fast and are required to execute the new sales coverage model. To aid you in selecting software, I've included a resource directory that lists a variety of software companies for you to review and select the ones that match your needs and budget best. Clearly, no sales and marketing department can exist today without utilizing the new technology that is available. This book is about how to use marketing communications (particularly direct mail, E-mail, and telemarketing) to develop, in combination with the salespeople, a new, more productive sales coverage model. That's it—plain and simple!

Sales Productivity Is Job Number One

The overriding goal is to improve sales productivity. So, what is sales productivity? On the revenue side of the equation, it's the ability to sell more products and/or services to as many customers as possible. On the cost side, it's the total number of dollars required to acquire, retain, and grow that customer revenue. While everyone involved understands this, frequently we attack the two sides of this equation separately and suffer the consequences. Here's what happens all too often:

Sales revenue not only sits atop the financial statement and is referred to as the "top line" but also is the primary driver of all the sales and marketing efforts. "Sell more" translates into customer acquisition efforts, frequently without regard to how many dollars are being consumed to acquire a customer. Marketing spends the limited budget and counts the responses or leads that are passed to sales. Sales, in turn, will try to sell anyone who will buy and is almost always rewarded on total revenue generated. Only rarely do you find companies that reward on the margin of the sale, and if so, it's usually only for certain products and services. Rarely, in my more than thirty-five years of sales and marketing experience, has the question been raised as to how much it was costing to acquire and keep customers. Everything was measured in revenue results. The ultimate example is, of course, the recent dot-com era, in which companies were spending far more money to acquire customers than the total revenue each customer would realistically generate in a one-, two-, or even five-year period. The odd thing was that most were aware of this imbalance but went ahead anyway. Their rationalization was the "built-to-flip" mentality, which was supported by the unrealistic valuations that the stock market was placing on these firms. We all know what happened to this business model.

On the cost side, we are all too familiar with how reductions in budgets or staff take place. Across-the-board or specific cuts are made to meet the need to "bring costs in line with revenue." Seldom is there a similar reduction in sales revenue based on a cut in the marketing or sales budget. When I was at IBM I learned a new way to deal with budget reductions and, in my mind, it was quite appropriate: if the marketing or sales manager's budget or resources had been cut too much, the manager could "de-commit" on his or her revenue objectives. While it sounded good, I don't know of anybody who actually de-committed, since to do so started a process that ended up at senior management levels, and nobody wanted to take that kind of career risk. So, budget and resource cuts were just accepted, and everyone just tried harder and hoped that we would make their revenue numbers.

In chemistry, when dealing with chemical reactions, the term *equilibrium* is used to denote the natural balance between both sides of an equation. Press too much on one side of the equation and it affects the other side. Much like a chemical reaction, there is a cause-and-effect relationship in this revenue/cost equation. Too much effort expended on the revenue side affects the cost, and likewise, cost cuts affect the revenue side. What is required is a better formula to find the right balance to produce the desired productivity result. This book is about finding the right balance, or equilibrium.

The Four Customer Life Cycle Phases

There are four commonly accepted phases of the customer life cycle:

- Customer acquisition
- Customer growth and retention
- Customer loyalty
- Customer reactivation

The old selling model was very linear. Marketing communications was primarily involved in customer acquisition by developing communications that generated inquiries. In recent years this included lead qualification as well. After that, the sales group took over and did everything else. In fact, if marketing was ever inclined to communicate to specific customers, the salespeople would get angry and tell marketing in no uncertain terms, "These are my customers, my territory, my job; so stay out!" Those days have been over for at least the last ten years; it's just that sales and management haven't realized it yet.

The new sales coverage model starts with the premise that in each of the four customer life cycle phases, a redesign of this linear approach is required to develop a more productive sales model based on the reality that salespeople can no longer do the "rest" of the job. There are four primary communications media that have the ability to both target an individual and initiate the contact. They are as follows, ordered from the lowest cost per contact to the highest:

E-mail:	$0.01–$0.10 each
Postal mail:	$0.50–$10+ each
Telephone call:	$20–$45+ each
Sales call:	$150–$1,200+ each

Descriptions of these media and their cost and effectiveness are covered later in this chapter.

It's these four targetable media that should be blended to contact and communicate to the potential and current customer base throughout all four phases of the customer life cycle. The first three are classic direct marketing media, and therefore, the integration is primarily between direct marketing and sales. Yes, there are certainly other useful marketing processes, such as public relations, advertising, trade shows, and event marketing, but they cannot be targeted to specific individuals. The appropriate split between using direct marketing and salespeople in each of the customer life cycle phases is a decision for you to make based on the go-to-market strategy unique to your company or industry. For guidance, Figure 2.1 provides a general perspective on how these media may divide the job of communicating and selling to prospective, current, and past customers.

A brief explanation is in order:

• **Customer acquisition** (60 percent direct marketing, 40 percent sales). The traditional role of direct marketing has been to generate inquiries, qualify leads, and pass the leads to sales for conversion. There's not much change here, assuming that a lead qualification and development program is in place for marketing to execute. The salesperson clearly should be involved in converting the sale and developing the initial cus-

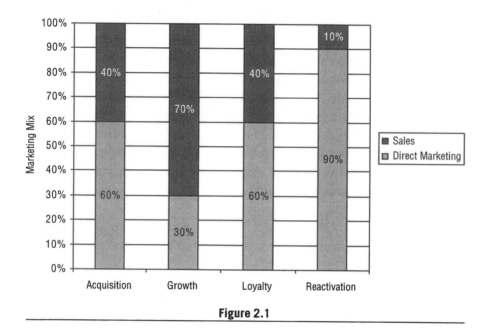

Figure 2.1

tomer relationship. Back in the late 1980s, McGraw-Hill reported that it took an average of 5.4 sales calls to close a sale. Most B2B sales experts contend that this number has increased significantly in the interceding years and is close to seven or eight today. The question to answer is, how many of these sales calls could be accomplished by direct marketing techniques today? Most companies with which I deal are trying to eliminate at least two or three calls in the customer acquisition phase. The activity of lead qualification and development results in marketing's handing over to salespeople opportunities that are far more qualified and ready to engage in a real purchase than in the old days. These calls are obviously the ones early in the acquisition effort, as it is unproductive for salespeople to not only make cold calls, but also qualify the inquiries as well. This represents an immediate improvement in sales productivity, as not only do salespeople have to make fewer calls to close a sale, but they also have freed up their time and sales calls that were devoted to the early customer acquisition calls for more productive sales calls on qualified leads or customers. Don't forget, salespeople have a finite number of sales calls they can make each year, and so a reduction of one call translates to one additional call (and hopefully it will be more productive).

- **Customer growth** (30 percent direct marketing; 70 percent sales). This phase of the customer life cycle is where the salesperson plays the most important role. Finding opportunities to up-sell or cross-sell and secure the customer relationship is best placed in the hands of the sales staff. At the same time, there is also a valid role for direct marketing to assume. The sales group should not call on every customer. In some cases, an inside sales telemarketing effort can team with outside sales to share the contact responsibility. This teaming can be very cost-effective while actually increasing the contact frequency for the customer. In addition, the salesperson should have identified other decision influencers who also may not be worth the direct sales effort but do need to receive relevant messages and offers from the company. Direct mail or E-mail can play an important role in communicating in a cost-efficient manner to the entire "decision tree" in the customer growth and retention phase.

- **Customer loyalty** (60 percent direct marketing; 40 percent sales). Salespeople can easily take the customer for granted, particularly one that presents no new sales opportunities in the future. In fact, in his book *Upside-Down Marketing* (McGraw-Hill, 1994), George Walther reports that 68 percent of "past customers" said that the reason they stopped buying from the supplier was that they didn't feel "loved" anymore. This response is a direct result of salespeople not keeping in contact. They probably didn't think they needed to or felt it was a waste of their time. So, without any other form of marketing communications, the customer felt neglected and stopped buying. This research was, of course, done during the time that salespeople didn't want or even allow marketing to communicate directly to their customers. Failing to keep in contact is a big mistake, as studies have indicated that, on average, 10 percent of the customer base decays each year. The latest quantification of this statistic was noted in Frederick Reichheld's book *The Loyalty Effect* (Harvard Business School Press, 1996). If extrapolated to a five-year period, then one-half of the current customer base would no longer be customers and would have stopped buying. Certainly a dramatic loss for any company. So the question has to be asked: how many of these customers would have "decayed" if better contact were maintained? That is why there is such a large role for direct marketing in the customer loyalty phase; highly targeted and relevant communications can keep up the contact.

In addition, as the life cycle of a customer matures to the loyalty phase, many new people and functions can be involved in the consumption of the product or service. Their user experience is based on the current product or service and, at times, this experience becomes "tired" or "old hat." Or new users arrive without the prior knowledge as to why this particular product or service was purchased in the first place. Without an ongoing communication program from the vendor to all the decision makers and influencers, these users frequently begin to look for a newer and improved version. This can lead directly to a lost customer, and the sad fact is that without ongoing contact, the customer is lost before it is even known that they are looking for a replacement. When an old customer "fires" you, it is a shocking experience and hard to explain to management.

• **Customer reactivation** (90 percent direct marketing, 10 percent sales). Not many companies focus on past customers even though, over time, they represent a larger and larger group. The salespeople, if new in the territory, may not even know that these companies have bought in the past. We all know that it is easier to sell current customers more products than it is to sell new customers. The same can be said for past customers—on average, it's easier to sell a past customer than a new one. What it takes is information on the past customer, verification of the appropriate contacts, as many have changed, and then a targeted campaign to reactivate old customers. There is a high probability that these customers know your company and product, so the role a salesperson assumes is minimized. A strong direct mail and telemarketing program will open up sales opportunities with many lapsed customers. Chapter 4 contains a great example of a campaign focused on past customers that proves the point.

Do Not Cover the Market by Size of Customer

One of the first efforts I see when companies start to redesign the sales coverage is to assign current customers to one of several "media" based on their revenue. Here's the typical breakdown:

• Small customers are covered by direct mail; they need to call the company to contact an inside salesperson or customer service. Nobody calls them!

- Medium-size customers are assigned to an inside salesperson and removed from the outside salesperson's territory responsibility.

- Larger accounts remain the responsibility of the field sales group.

This approach sounds so logical that it almost defies criticism. But scratch the surface a bit and companies find a number of errors in this structure. First, the decision to label a customer small, medium, or large is typically based on current sales revenue. That analysis ignores the potential revenue at stake and relegates the customer to, more than likely, always being either small or medium. A number of years ago, Roadway Express did just what is described here and split sales coverage by media of contact. I was asked to create a direct mail program to the small customer group. When I accepted the assignment and was given the large list of small customers, I was surprised to find that there were no names of people on the customer record. Under the circumstances, everyone agreed that we should send these companies a direct mailing with a value-based offer and ask for the name of the shipping/receiving manager. While designing the DM piece, we also included a question on how much freight the company shipped each year. Since the revenue cut to define small customers was $5,000 or less, we naively expected answers in that range. When the responses came back, and we did get an 8 percent response rate, almost 30 percent of the customers listed yearly freight volume in excess of $50,000—the definition for an A, or large customer, that was assigned to a field salesperson. What Roadway was missing was the "share-of-customer" view. Needless to say, these results spoke for themselves and changed the company's thinking on sales coverage. In this situation, a combined direct mail and telemarketing contact strategy was appropriate until the customer eventually grew. With just a direct mail effort, the potential for customer growth was all but eliminated.

Covering Large Accounts with Only a Salesperson Doesn't Work Either

On the other end of the spectrum is the very common approach to assign large accounts to salespeople. This even has gone to the level of establishing national account managers (NAMs) who are dedicated to one or several customers and tasked with the job of penetrating these accounts. Typically, the account is selected because of the current or potential sales revenue, and "it just makes sense to devote our best sales reps to these key accounts." Logic I will give you—effectiveness I will not. I speak from experience. When I was in sales for Quaker Oats Chemical, some of my "large accounts" were Ford, Goodyear, Chrysler, and 3M. There was no other contact or communications coming from Quaker—I was it! Well, in spite of the fact that I tried my best, I couldn't get to see everyone who was involved with the research, specification, and purchase of our chemicals. This was particularly true at 3M, where the purchasing department blocked you from calling on any other individuals in the company, as they wanted to filter and control the salespeople. I tried to circumvent this policy and had some success, but I was always in fear that the purchasing agent would find out and read me the riot act. 3M may not be still doing this today, but back when I was selling, I'm sure that we missed opportunities at 3M because I couldn't get to see or even talk to the right people. In other large-account situations, I didn't have enough time to see everyone, since I had five states and more than a hundred other accounts in the $5 million territory.

This problem has grown worse, as many of the individuals who would see salespeople in years past will not do so now. So, by turning over the sole contact responsibility to a salesperson, a company is all but ensuring that fewer people within these large accounts will be familiar with and supportive of the selling proposition. This situation has been exacerbated as organizations have moved more toward matrix or team management and the number of people involved in decision making or influencing has actually increased. In fact, one of the difficult facts faced by salespeople now is that larger companies are making their people "virtual." This means that decision makers and influencers may move assignments but not move locations. In addition, many employees work from their homes—not a place to conduct a sales call. I acknowledge that these people may see the advertising or stop by a trade show booth, but they have no personal and direct contact with the supplier. So, when another competitor enters the picture, there is no loyalty or well-understood value proposition related to the current supplier that keeps these people from switching.

When visiting clients and talking to them about their products or services, I frequently hear them extol the virtues of their offerings versus the competition. Yet, they are losing in the marketplace to these same competitors on a daily basis. What is occurring is that while they may, in fact, be better, they are not getting this message, or value proposition, through to all the right buyers because they are relying almost exclusively on their field people to "carry the mail." The solution to the problem rests with properly communicating to all the people on the "decision tree."

I'm not at all proposing that national account managers be pulled off the accounts. What I am saying is that their efforts need to be supplemented with other forms of direct communication to the individuals they identify with regard to their functional roles in the organization. This knowledge is recorded in a database and used to launch relevant communications to these individuals. In fact, the national account manager frequently directs the marketing communications group on content of message, timing, and media of delivery. This is really what customer relationship management is all about in B2B (more on CRM later), and the NAMs are the maestros of the CRM process for their accounts.

So, how would NAMs react to this type of coverage model in which they are not the only medium of communications? Typically, at first, they don't think it's a good approach, but when their defenses are down and they realize that they are not going to lose their jobs, they embrace it. They know, like all good salespeople, that they aren't getting through to all the contacts. Just this year I was giving an internal seminar on this approach at Square D, and Matt Douglas, OEM marketing manager, said, "My salespeople are sitting in the lobbies of chip manufacturers; the customers won't even see them when they show up!" Matt, you're not alone. All salespeople confront the problem of not being able to see key decision makers and influencers—and it's not the fault of the salespeople. It's just that fewer and fewer people are now receptive to spending time with salespeople.

The Dark Side of Traditional Sales Coverage

In the "old" days, when I was selling, the primary storage system for all of my customer information was "neck-up." Sure, I recorded names of contacts on the sales sheets I carried on each customer, and there were brief call reports in the file, but if I had been hit by a bus or left the company, the more personal "soft" information would have been lost, leaving the next salesperson at a great disadvantage. Today we rely on ACT or some other sales force automation (SFA) system, but basically the same information that appeared on those sales sheets is recorded.

More than once, I have heard clients moan about losing a salesperson and then subsequently losing business due to the lack of retained in-depth customer knowledge. I'm not talking about records of shipments or contact names; I am referring to "soft" information about the people and business situation specific to each customer. We all know the value of the knowledge and insight in the heads of good salespeople. Most, if not all, of this valuable resource left when the salesperson left, and the new one had to start all over. How do you think the customers felt when turnover occurred? Not good, as they had to educate the new salesperson on their business and history. Frequently, the customer just turned to the next supplier in line who had been attempting to get the business—and knew the people and business situation as a result. The relationship with the next supplier was able to leapfrog the old one because the "relationship" with the old supplier was totally tied up with the salesperson and not the company. The loss of business was almost assured if the former salesperson went to work for a competitor in the same territory or if the new sales rep didn't show up for several months due to the hiring and training process. While CRM is supposed to close the gap, it's not working (more on CRM later).

In *The Loyalty Effect*, Frederick Reichheld documents that, on average, companies lose 10 percent of their customers each year. What he doesn't say is why. While I've not done any quantitative study on this, my sales and sales management experience tells me that in B2B a large portion of customer decay is due to changes in salesperson coverage and the breaking of the established relationship. This disruption occurs not just when salespeople leave (when they quit or are fired) but also when companies change the sales assignments. It really doesn't matter to the customer why the salesperson is no longer there. What does matter is that these human relationships that have been built up over time are gone. A law of physics says that a vacuum will be filled. Well, loss of a salesperson causes a vacuum, and the customer will fill it—and likely with another relationship from a competitor.

So, how does the new sales coverage model bring us back from the "dark side"? In short, it develops a relationship with a customer that is broader than just the salesperson. This is not to say that it replaces the salesperson; it does not. Rather, it adds to the breath and depth of the relationship that customers feel they have with your company. This, in fact, may include another human relationship if your coverage model teams an inside salesperson with the field person. Not only is this new sales coverage model desired by the customer, but also it relieves the field person of having to make all the contacts and deliver all the required messages.

Building the Overall Customer Relationship

The new sales coverage model is intended to build customer relationships that go beyond the salesperson. Here are the salient characteristics of the model:

• Information regarding all the decision makers and influencers within a customer's organization is in a database, and relevant communications are sent to each person based on the person's role and involvement with the purchase. The number and subject of the communications vary; it's not about a deluge of mailings, E-mails, or phone calls. It is about properly timed and value-based messages—and the customer, not you, is the arbiter of the value of the message.

• All decision makers and influencers are familiar with your company, value proposition, and overall relationship as a supplier of products or services. They are informed and not in the dark.

• Customers have methods to contact or interface with your company other than through the salesperson. When they use one of these alternative methods—for example, inside sales or customer service—they are confident that this contact is relayed promptly to the salesperson. How often do we feel that the right hand of a company doesn't know what the left hand is doing? Of course, this holistic view requires one database of information shared by all customer contact groups.

• The number of sales calls will decline, but the frequency and total number of contacts will increase. The result is that the customer will feel better served and have a closer relationship with your company. Vic Hunter, of Hunter Business Direct, recounts the experience of Shell Oil, which teamed an inside salesperson with the current outside salesperson. During the course of the next year, the number of face-to-face calls, which had approximated eight to twelve, declined to four, while contacts by inside sales totaled ten to fifteen. At the end of the year when a survey of the customers' test base was taken, most of them could not remember who had made the last call (a testament to the inside salesperson) and felt far better served by Shell. Notice this was not a replacement of the outside salesperson but rather a supplement to the existing relationship that enhanced the satisfaction for the customer.

Sales Productivity Shoots Up

Here's an example of how sales productivity can shoot up just as a result of removing some of the call load that a typical sales group shoulders. A medical equipment supplier was experiencing flat sales, and my agency was hired to develop a direct marketing program to generate more sales leads. While in the process of creating the campaign, I asked to meet with some salespeople so that I could understand their lead needs more thoroughly. The Southern Region was selected, and I then traveled with several of the salespeople in Florida and also met with the regional manager, who was based in Orlando. What became most apparent when I accompanied the salespeople on a normal business day is that they were making an extremely wide array of calls, including delivering batteries to emergency medical units at firehouses—one of their products was a line of defibrillators. The rationale for battery delivery was that if the battery went out of date, there was a liability issue. This observation caused me to audit all the calls that the salespeople were making, and the total was thirteen different types of calls. When I asked how many of these calls they thought were the most important ones, the answer was only four. When I asked the regional manager the same question, he gave me the same four. The eight salespeople in the region were making nine types of calls, representing approximately 30 percent to 40 percent of their time, because they had no other option and no one to whom to turn for support. They were the sum total of customer contact in their territories, and while their core job description didn't include these activities, they were the only resource available to do the job.

Therefore, we began to figure out how these other activities could be handled by adding an inside person to team with them and remove this burden. The restructuring wasn't smooth or easy, but in six months, sales in the Southern Region began to increase far faster than other regions. The primary reason was that these eight salespeople now had more time to devote to more important potential and current customers; more time equated to more revenue. Here's how the numbers worked out:

> Total calls per month for each salesperson (20/week $\times$ 4 weeks) = 80 calls
> 20–30 percent reduction
> 16–24 calls now available for other sales opportunities
> 4 calls needed to make a sale worth $15,000 on average
> 4–6 more sales per month = $60,000–$90,000 per salesperson
> 8 salespeople $\times$ $60,000–$90,000 more each month = $480,000–$720,000 monthly increase
> Margin of 55 percent = incremental margin of $264,000–$396,000 per month
> Cost of 2 inside sales support people per month = $8,000

Not a bad return on the investment, by any standards. The sales increase that began to appear in six months far exceeded management's expectations, and the company quickly realized that by freeing up the salespeople's time with inside support, they could achieve a quick 20 percent increase in revenue. In addition, the salespeople were enthusiastic, as they didn't have to make these low-priority types of calls anymore. I think it can be said with no fear of contradiction that good salespeople want to sell and not waste time. Yet, with so many of the traditional sales models, salespeople make many calls that are just not productive. They do it primarily because there is no other direct communication from the company to the customer, and they feel a strong sense of responsibility to their customers. Yes, we did institute a lead program, but that was icing on the cake.

The Positives and Negatives of the Three Direct Marketing Media

Direct mail, E-mail, and the telephone are different media. Not only do they require different capabilities to launch, but they also have unique impacts on the receiver.

Let's briefly examine each in the context of the new sales coverage model.

Direct Mail

The most traditional of the three direct marketing media is direct mail. It's so common that one of its most endearing attributes is that people rarely get upset when they receive a piece of mail. The primary negative attribute is that it's easy to ignore: a flick of the wrist over the wastebasket does the trick for most people. Another feature of direct mail that makes it such an effective medium is that it is tactile and visual—we touch it and look at it. E-mail and telephone communications are more fleeting. The tactile nature of this medium gives it an "impact" aspect that is important, particularly if the package goes "bump" in the mail. The great advantage of B2B over consumer programs is that the value of the sale is so much higher. As a result, we can frequently afford to send boxes, tubes, or lumpy envelopes containing some promotional item, all of which will be opened and read at a higher rate than a "flat" mailing. In addition, we can be more creative than in E-mail and telephone contact, even though E-mail is catching up by using streaming media, flash, and PDF formats.

One of the big problems with mail is that other people handle and even screen it before it reaches the target. Getting through the mail room, particularly in large companies, is difficult if the item is not accurately addressed or is sent third class. Believe it or not, some large companies have authorized their mail rooms to throw out third-class mail if they are overloaded and can't get to all the mail. If you work in a large company, go to the mail room and see what actually happens. It will give you a deeper appreciation of how direct mail is handled.

In years past, we used the term *gatekeeper* to refer to the secretary or administrative assistant who received the mail for the boss and was frequently empowered to sort the correspondence and discard what was not appropriate for that individual. Today we don't have as many of these gatekeepers except at the "C" level (CEO, COO, CFO, et cetera). That's an improvement if you're not targeting these individuals, but if you are, consideration must be given to getting through the gatekeeper. Several years ago, one of my good friends, Ron Jacobs, of Jacobs and Clevenger in Chicago, told me of a very effective mailing campaign sent to the presidents of large companies. On top was a mailing to the administrative assistant (they had called first to obtain his or her name). It was a personal note with a paperweight and a "thank-you" for ensuring that the mailing was seen by the person's boss. While this may appear as a bribe, it worked, and the follow-up phone call got through more than 70 percent of the time.

Another enemy of direct mail is the inbox. We all know the volume of mail that comes in each day and, if we're gone for a day or two, the high stack that greets us when we return. Here, lumpy is also good, as it frequently doesn't even find the inbox and instead sits next to it or even on the desk or chair. There are numerous techniques to fight through the inbox. Another one is to design the mailing piece as though it's a personal business communication. A closed-face envelope of quality stock with your company logo, a laser-printed address block, and a first-class stamp will do the trick. This letter will get opened, as it appears that it is an important communication compared with all the self-mailers, catalogs, and poorly designed mail surrounding it in the inbox. There's much more to designing a direct mail package, and I'll leave it to the experts to help you further, as my focus here is how to get the communication seen and read by the targeted individual.

E-Mail

If I had written this book a year ago, my enthusiasm for E-mail would have been much greater. Unfortunately, this medium is fast self-destructing and losing its effectiveness. I'm not saying that Web or interactive marketing is not key to our overall marketing strategies; it is, and it will grow in importance. I'm talking only about E-mail sent to those on a company's permission list. By the way, I fully support Seth Godin and his philosophy as so well articulated in his book *Permission Marketing* (Simon & Schuster, 1999). He is absolutely right when he states that the only E-marketing is to have someone's permission to send E-communications. So, my starting point is that we have obtained the permission of all individuals in our database to whom we communicate by E-mail. Do not send E-mail to those who have not, in some fashion, opted in. Spam in B2B is detrimental to the new sales coverage model and to overall prospect and customer relationships.

The problem is rather simple: everyone is using E-mail because it doesn't cost much to launch a communication to a large number of individuals. Its appeal doesn't stop there, either. I've done a number of E-mail campaigns in which the time from conception to measurement spanned one or two weeks and not the months it takes for a direct mail program to be developed, mailed, and measured. Quite a drug for a direct marketer—once you do it, it can become habit-forming. And that's the hitch. The habit is becoming an addiction. We all can confirm the truth of that statement when we open the E-mail box every morning. Talk about an overflowing inbox! Of course, we have caused some of this overflow ourselves by happily subscribing to E-newsletters, accepting updates from industry vendors, allowing our names to be included on distribution lists, and similar actions. I'm not aware of a current study on the number of E-mails received in B2B, but, as noted earlier, other studies have indicated that more than 70 percent of unrecognized or unwanted E-mail messages are instantly deleted. This percentage is growing fast and may soon approach 100, just based on the exponential growth in clutter. Even among those who have opted in, there is a high probability that if your dialogue with them has not been recent, they also will delete your message immediately, since people's memories may not be able to retain all the companies and Web communications to which they said yes.

While deletion is a problem, another is that, unlike with postal mail, some people become upset when they receive E-mails that they did not request or that are sent from someone they don't know. This reaction appears to be based on a feeling of invasion of privacy that individuals harbor with E-mail but not postal mail. "How did they get my name and E-mail address?" is a refrain that is heard frequently. Another anomaly is that the negative response to E-mail is much higher among Internet-savvy or younger individuals, as they seem to have a proprietary feeling about this medium. The negative reactions can take the form of what are called "flaming" E-mails. Here's an example. Last year we worked with Sales Logix, a maker of sales force automation software—their brand names are ACT and Sales Logix. The company had a list of people who had viewed a Web demo of the Sales Logix software—real leads, not just inquiries. Sales Logix sent an E-mail to this segment of the prospect database offering a white paper that was an evaluation of SFA software by an independent consulting organization. Pat Sullivan, the president of Sales Logix, got five flaming E-mails from recipients complaining that he had no right to communicate to them. This wasn't even a selling message! Certainly, there is a cultural element to online marketing that must be carefully considered before marketing communications are launched.

Telephone or Telemarketing

Probably no other medium evokes more emotion than the word *telemarketing*. At parties, when asked what I do, I never imply that my job involves or even comes close to telemarketing, as I know that what would follow would not be pleasant. Nevertheless, in my effort to develop effective marketing communication campaigns for clients, I deploy telemarketing daily. There are many reasons to integrate telemarketing in B2B, and in the new coverage model it is an irreplaceable medium. We're not talking about the kind of telephone calls you get just when you're sitting down to dinner that are tightly scripted and are obvious telemarketing calls. In B2B that style will not work, as businesspeople are far less tolerant of these calls than consumers are, if you can believe it. The only way telemarketing will fit into the new sales coverage model is by assuming the form and format of an important business discussion. The caller is conversational and knowledgeable, and the message is not obviously scripted. While the telemarketers are following what is called a "loose script," they don't speak verbatim, which would lead to disconnects both literally and figuratively. Here are the reasons that telemarketing is a primary element of the new sales coverage model:

- It's a human interface, unlike mail and E-mail. In the early 1900s Josiah Royce at Harvard performed the first studies on human loyalty. His findings are important in building customer loyalty and are discussed more thoroughly in Chapter 8. He found that our foremost loyalty is to humans, followed by other groups and morals. Since salespeople are not now seen or received as often by customers, there is a need to replace this human contact with other forms of personal contact to create relationships and loyalty. Telemarketing is the primary medium to achieve this goal. Of course, a variety of degrees of relationship can be created over the phone, as limited as a call from someone you don't know and to whom you will never speak again, and as intensive as contact with an inside salesperson to whom you talk daily or weekly. No matter what the degree of relationship is, it is a *person* on the phone, and we react to that fact alone. One of the ways to make the outreach even more personal is for telemarketers or inside salespeople who routinely talk to a customer to include their pictures on the letterhead or business cards they send to the customer. Having a picture of the person to whom you're talking can do wonders for establishing a relationship.

• Because this is a dynamic medium based on a dialogue, the conversation can lead in many directions. A response to a mailing or E-mail, no matter how well structured, is not a dialogue. Therefore, the productivity obtainable with a good conversation is far greater than with the other two media. On the other hand, it does not replace a face-to-face sales call in its impact and never will. You quickly find this out if you try to write a loose script for a telemarketing campaign: even the simplest of objectives requires many splits in the script based on the prior answer given. The best script is, in fact, no script at all. That assumes that the caller is fully trained in the product or service and represents your company full-time. Inside salespeople are examples of this type of "no-script" caller.

• The number of calls that can be made each day far outstrips the number of possible field sales calls. That's obvious, but have you ever calculated the productivity of a telemarketing effort versus the sales effort? Granted, the impact is not the same, but let's just look at the numbers:

> Field sales calls per day = 3
> Completed telemarketing calls per day = 8*

Now let's look at the cost side:

> Sales call = $200 to $500+
> Telemarketing call = $30 to $75

It's obvious that a soundly based telemarketing effort is cost-efficient and needs to be part of the overall sales model.

• Finally, potential and current customers frequently prefer a phone call to a sales visit. That's a hard pill to swallow for guys like me who grew up in sales, but it's true today. This preference has two drivers. First is availability. A person sitting at a phone is much more available than a person in the field. Cell phones have made a difference in being able to contact a field salesperson, but this method isn't satisfactory when the person is in a meeting, on an airplane, or otherwise not available to answer the phone. An inside sales or customer service group is a highly valued attribute of your overall service level to customers. The second

---

*A completed call is defined as one that reaches the intended individual and meets the goal of the call. It is not a dial, callback, or partial complete. This average was provided by Businesslink, in Des Moines, Iowa, a firm that specializes in B2B telemarketing.

driver is time conservation. Clearly, if it takes only a phone call to move the buying process forward, determine if the product or service fits a need, or accomplish some other such purpose, then a phone call in the era of "time shortage" today is far preferable.

There are many types of telemarketing efforts, and many fine B2B telemarketing firms, consultants, and books dot the landscape. The Resource Directory at the end of this book lists a range of telemarketing help. At IBM we divided the roles of telemarketing into the following four functional categories:

• **Inbound call centers.** A call center received phone requests stimulated by our marketing communications. Different phone numbers and/or extensions were used for different campaigns so that callers quickly got to the proper person who could help answer questions and fulfill their requests. This function was outsourced.

• **Lead qualification telemarketing.** When an inquiry was received from any of a number of sources, an outbound call was placed to determine if the inquiry was qualified to move to the next stage of the buying process and the next level of IBM sales resource. This staff was a combination of outsourced and internal employees who were on contract.

• **Lead nurturing telemarketing.** Frequently, the inquiry was a potential lead for sales but not yet ready to be handed off. We didn't want to lose the sales opportunity, so we kept it alive with periodic calls from this group. I never liked the term *nurturing*, so later in the book you'll see this activity defined as *lead development*. These telemarketers were IBM employees, as their skill set needed to be at a higher level.

• **Inside sales.** Our most effective and costly telemarketing or telesales group was sometimes known as the "sharks" in an affectionate way. This group received qualified leads that were not appropriate for coverage by field sales or business partners. These highly skilled, motivated, and paid individuals sold more hardware and software than IBM management thought possible.

There have been two recent developments in telemarketing. The first has been started in the last several years and has proved to be very effective. Simply, it's the use of outbound telemarketing to create leads on a per-lead cost basis. Here's the deal: firms such as Q-Genesis, Lead Dogs, and

Protocol will call a cold list of companies who are within your targeted potential customer base and develop leads that meet your criteria. They are paid either on a per-hour or a pay-for-performance model. People who feel that cold calling is a thing of the past are often shocked when real leads are handed over and result in sales. Many of these firms are referenced in the Resource Directory.

Second, a new automated form of call messaging has been developed by SoundBite. This approach either leaves a message on the voice mail of the target or, if the person answers, has a voice-interactive capability that allows for an interaction. This new technique has been used successfully to obtain re-ups for qualified magazine subscriptions and to leave a message that a direct mailing is on the way. All direct marketers are looking to increase response rates, and a carefully timed telephone call can bump the number of responses. Another application of this voice-activated technique is for data updating, as the data decay rate is high in B2B and it is expensive to call with "live" operators and determine the proper individual who should receive the subsequent communication. This technology can easily record information on who holds a specific position within a company.

What About Other Media?

Other marketing communications media are considered "surround sound" in the new sales coverage model. They all have value in an overall marketing campaign; it's just that they cannot pinpoint and communicate to specific individuals with the accuracy and timing of direct mail, E-mail, and telemarketing. The following sections briefly discuss how to view each of the other marketing communications media in the context of this new perspective.

Public Relations

In B2B most public relations efforts are directed to obtaining mentions in trade journals of new products or services. These mentions can be a great source of inquiries, if the PR release regarding the product or service includes an offer and a method to respond. If the offer is just a brochure, make it sound like a great brochure worth the effort to obtain one. Frequently, these offers and methods of response will find their way into the magazine and will help generate inquiries. The second most frequent use of PR is attempting to obtain mentions in articles that the magazine editors are writing or even suggesting articles penned by a company technical expert or senior executive. While having the article published may feel good and make the author's ego jump a notch or two, the real value is using the reprints in a direct marketing program. More mileage will come from this usage than from the publication of the article. The key benefit of having an article as part of a direct-mailing campagn is the implied third-party credibility it brings to the product or service. We face a very skeptical marketplace, and anything that can be presented to a potential or even current customer that endorses the product or service goes a long way toward reducing this skepticism, and therefore will increase readership and response rates.

Under certain circumstances, a local PR effort will also pay great dividends. Here are two situations that demand a local PR effort. The first is if the firm has most, if not all, of its customer base in a concentrated geographic area. For instance, a commercial bank concentrates geographically, and coverage by the local media will be quite important to distinguish one bank from another, assuming that the PR is good. Secondly, if a geographic sales blitz is part of the plan, then a local PR effort may be far more cost-effective than a similarly targeted advertising campaign. Recently, one of our clients desired to geographically expand their customer base for 401(k) plans and were targeting companies with between 25 and 100 employees. In Phoenix there were approximately 5,200 firms in this size range. PR was used in place of a paid advertising effort to reach those firms just before a direct mail campaign was begun. Response rates were substantially above the expected and several respondents even mentioned the PR effort.

The only negative to PR is that the message can't be fully controlled, as it can with advertising. Many a client has been upset about a negative story and errors that occur in the article. It's even happened to me. Last year we did a great campaign that was featured in *Direct* magazine. Good PR, to be sure, except that the reporter incorrectly said we were in Tucson, not Phoenix. I have no idea how many leads we lost because of his carelessness. PR is good; just don't count on it too much.

Advertising

Talk about sacred cows! Advertising is what marketing communications was all about not more than ten years ago. Creating ads and fielding the inquiries that came in from "bingo" cards was a career for many and a great income stream for ad agencies. I like advertising: it looks pretty, can be funny, has interesting headlines, and allows trade magazines to stay in business so that once in a while I am able to tear out a thought-provoking or important article. All good stuff, to be sure, but not cost-effective for the new sales coverage model. Frankly, I'd rather take the several thousand dollars that an ad costs to create and run and use that money to send a high-impact direct mail piece or launch a telemarketing effort. At the end of the day, I will wager that my expenditure of money will result in more leads and sales than the advertising, even if the ad generates good response. I don't want to sound too negative; it's just that I see a great waste of money today in B2B advertising campaigns at the expense of more-targeted communications. Brand or company awareness is good and has been proved to lift the response of direct marketing programs. I like that, but at what expense does it come? There is a balance to be struck between advertising effectiveness and blind repetition of the budget expenditures year after year based on the belief that our advertising is working. Don't forget that I'm an old salesperson, and I want results in terms of leads and sales—not just awards.

Therefore, I've become a fan of a slightly different perspective on traditional brand or awareness advertising. It's called "brand response," and it melds the characteristics of both brand advertising and response advertising. Here's the crux of the issue. Advertising agencies truly want to create memorable advertising; it looks great, but to coin a phrase, it's "less filling." Response rates are low. The ad looks great but does not drive behavior. No matter how many awards the ad wins, someone in management will ask the killer question: "So how many leads did we get?" Unfortunately, the answer is either "We don't know" or "We got lots of inquiries." Of course, inquiries are not leads. On the other side of the world are direct response agencies that design ads to drive behavior, not to win awards. As a result, the offer—and not the product—usually becomes the focus of the ad, and large 800 numbers and coupons appear. These ads will not win any awards, but they will drive responses. Unfortunately, the brand image and positioning usually suffers, so the brand value of these ads is low.

Brand response advertising merges these two different perspectives to create an ad that accomplishes both. My good friend Richard Rosen of AlloyRed in Portland has been a leading proponent of this approach, and practices it not only faithfully but with great success. If you want or need to create advertising, use brand response as your guiding light.

Trade Shows

We now come to the boondoggle of all the expenditures in the marketing communications budget. Trade shows can be good, but like Peck's bad boy, when they are bad, they are very, very bad (and costly, to boot!). One of the most desirable and toughest goals of participating in a trade show is to develop leads. You hear that objective stated as the primary reason for going to the show. At least it's a better rationale than the familiar "If we don't go, our competitors will say we're out of business." Boy, is that lame marketing justification or what! If the show is highly targeted to your primary market or segment, then go, and if you do, go in force. This means that a pre- and postshow marketing effort is launched to reach people on the preshow attendance list as well as those who stopped by your booth and grudgingly gave you their names. Of course, this pre- and postshow communication is a direct marketing one to give you the best chance to generate booth visits and postshow leads, respectively. I used to give seminars on trade show marketing and have been responsible for more shows than I want to remember. After every show, some senior manager (like my boss) would ask the dreaded question, "So, what did we get for our money at the last XYZ show?" My answers were frequently a great work of fiction. I would crow about the leads, comment on how well our salespeople did (if they even showed up for booth duty), note that we looked better than our competitors, and even suggest that this year's show was better than the last one—whatever that meant. He would smile, knowing that I was adding all the spin I could to justify my job. OK, enough bashing of trade shows. The point is that this is another marketing communications expenditure that frequently could be better applied.

One of my best stories concerning trade shows comes from my first days at IBM. I joined the company in November of 1994 and was informed that the direct marketing group would be quickly receiving the trade show leads from Comdex—that famous and gigantic computer show in Las Vegas. That year, unlike years past, IBM had decided to try to qualify leads on the show floor, and Tom Figgett, one of our direct marketing people, had teamed with IBM show management to set up the lead qualification procedures and forms to use at Comdex. A good start, all agreed. Soon enough, the several thousand leads came in, and we sent them to the lead qualification tele-sales group. We all had high expectations, knowing that the salespeople at the booth had been organized and trained to engage and qualify the thousands of individuals who stopped by the multimillion-dollar booth. In effect, these names were the real cream of Comdex, and for the first time we would track and measure sales opportunities that came from the show. Previously, all show contacts were sent to the sales groups based on the product or service checked on the form. No tracking or collecting feedback had ever been done. Now, given this unprecedented opportunity, the telemarketing group jumped in with both feet, since we didn't want the leads to "cool off."

As the reports began to arrive on my desk, I had to wonder if we had been sent the wrong box, as the telemarketing group uncovered almost no sales opportunities. I was receiving anxious calls from the sales groups who were expecting these opportunities to be passed to them. I got nervous; this was my first month on the job, and results didn't look good. It got so bad that I began to ask some questions of those who went to Comdex, and I uncovered the "smoking gun." The night before Comdex kicked off, one of the senior IBM people at the show had gathered everyone together and, in classic IBM fashion, instituted a sales contest for the salesperson or persons who qualified the most leads during the show. I don't recall the actual prize, but it was something like a week in Hawaii for you and your spouse. Well, being a former salesperson not inclined to shy away from any form of contest or competition, I can tell you that if I had found an attendee who got even close to the booth and fogged a mirror—the person was a "lead." When we called these people, a common response was, "All I wanted was a brochure—why are you calling me?" Only ten or so sales opportunities were found in the several thousand "leads," and the effort, along with Comdex, was judged a failure to generate sales opportunities. Several years later, IBM announced that it was withdrawing from Comdex and put the computer industry, and particularly the Comdex people, in shock. I don't know all the rationale behind this decision, but I bet the failure to produce real sales opportunities in 1994 had some direct bearing on it.

Seminars

I include seminars as a medium even though that definition may be a bit odd. The reason is that the attributes of seminars are unique, whether the sessions are presented in person or online. Attendees expect to receive information of value and have also made a real commitment. I really like seminars, as they are a drawing card to seriously interested buyers. Here are some thoughts and observations on seminars:

• A good seminar full of "information of value" is a strong offer to use in direct marketing campaigns. It fits the need for offers that make sense for lead qualification and development. Individuals do understand and will accept the fact that you will give a commercial message during the seminar, but be careful: don't focus the seminar on your sales pitch, which may turn off attendees more than attract customers. The use of an outside expert is strongly recommended, as the presentation then takes on an aura of credibility that internal people will never be able to project.

• If the seminar is given in person, some real advantages are created in the degree of personal contact that is possible. Just don't let your sales-people buttonhole the attendees too aggressively, as this is another real turnoff. Having a videotape of the seminar that can be sent to those who didn't show or couldn't make it will greatly extend the cost-effectiveness of the effort. Live seminars are expensive in both marketing and site costs, so use the event well. The video can even become an offer in a direct marketing campaign if the information is timeless. The seminar can also be put on CD, as more and more people prefer this media to video.

• We now have some great new software capabilities to hold seminars or demos online. Web-Ex and PlaceWare are two resources for online capabilities with potential and current customers. This is a great sales productivity tool, since salespeople can conduct the sessions from their offices. In addition, it is a tremendous time-saver for attendees. However, having given a number of online seminars, I need to issue a caveat: if a group of people have signed up, don't be surprised if half of them do not show up at the appointed time. It's easy to say yes and then not attend. Sending hard copies of the presentation on CD extends the value of the online seminar. I believe that online seminars have not reached their potential in the new sales coverage model, and in future years we will see a dramatic increase in new uses, as sales and marketing people become more comfortable with this form of virtual contact. There is certainly a huge cost savings attached in the "one selling to many" benefit of web seminars.

• Finally, there may be many opportunities for individuals from your company to speak at industry conferences or events. Take advantage of the public stage as much as you can. Leads will come from the audience, and tapes or copies of the presentation are valuable as offers to people not in attendance. In fact, most of my consulting business has been generated by just such a strategy: I've given twenty to twenty-five seminars and presentations each year for the last ten-plus years.

There are other media that, at times, may be considered, but I think that my point is clear. In the new sales coverage model, the traditional resources and budgets should be focused on direct mail, E-mail, and telemarketing if you want to achieve ever-increasing sales productivity improvements. Don't forget that all the proactive communications need to be recorded on a campaign management system so that when responses occur you can track back to see what's working. Of course, all the inquiries, leads, and sales opportunities are also recorded, and eventually a deep marketing database of prospects and customers will be developed. This gives me a great transition into the next section.

Customer Relationship Management

CRM has certainly been a hot topic in the last several years. Ask ten people what CRM means and it's likely you'll get ten different answers, if not more. I first heard the term at Texas Instruments, and it was defined by McKinsey (the company's consultant at the time) as "customer relationship marketing." This definition never caught hold, but in retrospect, maybe it should have, as what customer of yours wants to be "managed"? In my brief life on this planet, my experience has been that customers manage you—they call the tune, and you dance. OK, I'll get over it.

While I think that some of the concepts of CRM are great, I've always had a hard time understanding how this was different from advanced database marketing. Sure, the term was sexier, but in the end, it didn't seem any different to me or, I might add, to many of my colleagues, from what we'd been striving to achieve with database marketing. Unfortunately for the CRM software vendors, the proponents got off to a horrible start. First, it was all about technology: buy this or that software and you had CRM. What a bunch of baloney, as no marketing or sales software ever made a sale, to my knowledge. Then it was about the process of managing your customers, and that sounded a little better, but here again, they missed the boat—a different boat.

In late 2000 I attended a three-day conference on B2B CRM in Orlando, and since I felt behind the curve in this area, I went to as many sessions as possible to learn at the feet of experts. I did learn, but not what I was expecting. The speakers, all self-proclaimed experts in CRM, talked as though they had never met a real customer face-to-face, as their theories as to what would work were based on sending only E-mail communications! Shall we agree now that this view is a bit stilted? Maybe this explains why my E-mail inbox is overflowing each day. Another odd thing happened on my way to CRM heaven: not one person during the three-day event said the words *inquiry*, *lead*, or *qualified lead*. It was as though customers magically appeared with little or no effort. The really odd part of this is that we all know that first impressions are the strongest. This is particularly true in B2B, since the process of acquiring a customer can be quite involved for both the seller and buyer. There is no doubt that this process will create a substantial impression, if not a relationship, with the individuals who are making the buying decision—before a customer is created. Well, if CRM is all about managing customers, do we have a separate process to get them? In fact, I have recently begun to hear the term *prospect relationship management*, or PRM, as the precursor to CRM. I've not heard it from the CRM software companies but rather from smart marketers on the agency and client side.

I believe the view of CRM is now clear. It's the combination of technology (software and databases), the marketing and selling process, and the people charged with this responsibility. Almost all failures have revolved around process and people, as companies installed CRM software but didn't change either their marketing or selling processes or train the people charged with these responsibilities. In B2B, another key factor in CRM failure is the "dirty" data that underlies the system. No matter how good the technology, process, and people, if inaccurate information exists the results will not meet expectations. I take up the subject of "dirty" data later in this book, as in B2B the data accuracy and decay rate is so much worse than in the consumer realm that it completely changes the odds of CRM working at all.

It's no wonder that in 2002, The Gartner Group has reported that more than 65 percent of all CRM initiatives have failed (this includes both consumer and B2B). The primary reasons were that they cost way too much and they didn't produce sales results or improve customer satisfaction. Isn't it ironic that in the face of billions of dollars being spent on CRM in the last five years, national surveys show that customer satisfaction levels have trended downward and not up? I guess this proves Gartner's point.

I do support the premise that all customer contacts and interfaces should be recorded on a database and that this knowledge should be used to drive more relevant communications to these individuals. That will work and is the underlying technology needed to execute the new sales coverage model. What I do not support is the notion that all the communications be E-mail, which is what most CRM systems and strategies promote. Somehow we got sidetracked into thinking that everyone wants to be communicated to on the Internet. I strongly disagree. In B2B the variety and type of communications between a supplier and customer must be more robust to truly forge the relationships desired by both parties.

There is some value in thinking along the lines of CRM, but in B2B it will not meet the "sell more" and "spend less" goals. It is a part of the overall solution, not the entire solution.

Of all the marketing and sales issues of the last several years, CRM has been the most written and talked about of all. As CRM has been so beaten to death, this book is not a rehash of CRM principles. Rather, it presents a new way to look at this process: namely, a new way to look at your go-to-market strategy or, in other words, your new sales coverage model.

So, What Does the New Sales Coverage Model Look Like?

There are so many types of B2B selling situations that one "model" will not fit all. To demonstrate the variety, Figure 2.2 charts several characteristics of B2B selling situations and transactions and broadly suggests the most common communication tactic. The sections that follow explain the key parameters to identify to help determine the optimal coverage model for your company and/or market segment.

Nature of Product/Service Solution and Lead Time to Ship/Service

- **Commodity.** The product or service is widely available, has few distinctions, and is sold mainly on price and availability features. Office supplies and long-distance services are examples. The time to deliver is immediate, and if one supplier's offering is not available, the customer will buy the competitive solution.

- **Customized.** To meet customers' needs, something must be done to the product or service. Adding a custom color to a standard plastic and customizing fields in a software program are examples. Time to deliver is not immediate but must meet industry norms—usually from a week to a month.

- **Designed.** The product or service needs to be engineered or designed to meet customer needs. Machine tools and advertising agency services are examples. The lead time is long, and in some cases, the product or service requires multiple modifications before final delivery.

Degree of Relationship Desired/Needed Combined with Dollar Amount

- **Order ship.** This is an off-the-shelf product or service. When ordered, it is delivered without delay. No real relationship or contract between the customer and vendor need exist for this low-dollar purchase. Typically, such purchases are handled by one or two buyers within the customer's organization.

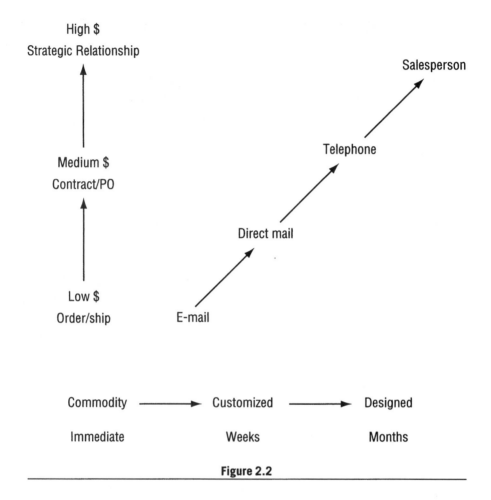

Figure 2.2

• **Contract or open purchase order.** To obtain the product or service at favorable terms, a contact or open PO needs to be negotiated. The relationship revolves around the negotiation, supply, and service of the item. The contract can be for a large dollar amount. Several people in the customer's organization may be involved, since specification, trial, approval, and ongoing servicing are all part of the sale.

• **Strategic relationship.** The nature of the product or service requires that a deep and long-lasting relationship be developed between the customer and supplier. This may involve engineering, top management, product management, and so forth. The dollar amount is measured not only in yearly revenue but also in lifetime value.

A brief comment on lifetime value here. Pragmatically, the lifetime value should not be stretched beyond a three-to-five-year period, since in most companies nobody will buy into a lifetime value that extends beyond this timeframe. Yes, many customers buy for more than five years (if not decades), but the amount of revenue will then be so high that the credibility of the number will be challenged. The real purpose of a lifetime value calculation is to cause everyone to keep an eye on the big picture, or what's really at stake for the company. This helps offset the at-times-unrealistic focus on meeting quarterly and yearly numbers.

The graph in Figure 2.2, of primary contact media versus transaction type, is intended to help you gain some insight into where you are in relation to the most likely primary media of coverage for any type of product or nature of the customer relationship. This is just a guideline to define the most likely primary media of contact. Other contact media should be part of the overall mix as you determine the sales coverage model that best fits your market situation.

Developing the Proper Blend of Contact Media

There is no magic formula for determining the ideal blend of contact media and the number of contacts to develop the new sales coverage model. While Figure 2.2 is a guideline as to which media may be employed the most frequently, the choice depends on your situation. Clearly, if you're selling office products (for example, Staples, Office Depot, Office Max), the media will be primarily E-mail, catalogs, and telephone. The salesperson is usually store-bound unless the size of the account or depth of relationship is high enough to justify a field salesperson. One way to look at blend of media is to assess the current cost of sales coverage and calculate a less costly model while at the same time increasing contact frequency and depth. Here's a simple example:

Current sales coverage
6 field sales calls per year at $250 each = $1,500 total coverage
   cost

2 people seen each visit on average = 12 contacts per year
Cost: $1,500   Contacts: 12

New coverage model
3 field sales calls per year at $250 each = $750:
   2 people per visit = 6 contacts
12 direct mailings at $5 each = $60: 12 contacts
12 telemarketing calls at $30 each = $360: 12 contacts
Cost: $960   Contacts: 28

Result
Cost reduced from $1,500 to $960
Number of contacts increased from 12 to 28 per year
Salesperson has 4 calls to use for other potential or current
   customers

I'm not at all implying by the preceding example that one direct mail piece or even a phone call is equal to one sales visit—it is not. On the other hand, the salesperson doesn't reach all the decision makers or influencers either. The direct mail and phone calls will reach others in the account, and so there is a trade-off between the impact of the contacts and the depth of the contacts. I've helped companies build fairly complex grids as a planning tool for a specific new coverage model, and I recommend that you develop them as well. It's just that there is no standard formula to apply. Many of these tactical decisions are dependent on the many variables found in B2B marketing and sales situations.

Summary

The main point of this book is that a new sales coverage model must be developed for your company for two driving reasons. First, greater sales and marketing productivity and effectiveness must be achieved to meet ever-increasing revenue goals and cost constraints. Second, if you don't do this and your competitor does, there is a great chance that the competitor will win in the marketplace. The new sales coverage model is a sustainable competitive advantage if you move fast. In five years from today, it will be the standard way companies organize to "go to market." Don't get left behind!

3

The Start: Profiling and Targeting the Market

IN THE SUMMERS of my college years I would visit my grandmother in Columbus, Ohio, and would get up early each morning and go to her country club—Scioto (that's where Jack Nicklaus learned to play golf)— to swim. I was a budding member of the swim team at Miami University (Ohio) and needed all the pool time I could get. The head lifeguard was Ron O'Brian, the top diver at Ohio State, and in those days, OSU had the best divers in the country. As you may expect, there was usually nobody around the club early in the day, so I would swim laps and Ron would practice his dives. He would try new ones for his upcoming senior season, and I watched in amazement as he got up on the ten-foot board, tried something like a three-and-a-half forward somersault with two twists, and—you guessed it—landed flat and hard! (From the ten-foot board the water feels like cement if you hit it wrong.) Just watching it gave me pain. So, one day I asked him what he was thinking when he tried new dives. He laughed a bit and gave me one of the best pieces of advice I ever received: "Well, John," he said, "if you put your head in the right position, your body soon follows!" Clearly, Ron had learned that the secret to a successful dive was keeping his head in the right position, making everything about this difficult physical movement seem easier.

I feel the same advice applies to marketers. When we develop campaigns or other tactical events, we frequently miss the mark and land hard. Profiling and targeting combined with the segmentation process is our "head position," and if we get it right, our marketing "body" will soon follow—and so much more easily! By understanding our current success, and then targeting the best future markets, we set ourselves up for a good "dive" and hopefully a good score. Ron knew just a bit about diving: the following year, he won both the low- and high-board NCAA championships for Ohio State. But we know him best as the Olympic diving coach of gold medal–winner Greg Louganis and other Olympians.

The reason I believe this process is so important is that in B2B much of the marketing planning and execution is done with little information or according to anecdotal input. It's not uncommon to have a company "identify" a target market and launch a program that is based only on several sales successes. Everyone gets excited and charges off to call on more of these "kinds of companies" without further analyzing the overall market to see if, in fact, that is a segment worth enough to target. As we move from sales-driven strategies to more integrated ones, there needs to be a much more disciplined method of targeting and segmentation. Overall, it's a three-step process:

- **Profiling:** Where are you now?
- **Targeting:** Where should you go?
- **Segmentation:** Who's going to get you there?

This chapter deals with profiling and targeting, which are important steps. Market segmentation is so critical to the new sales coverage model that it is treated in its own chapter, which follows. Companies that have not yet undertaken this three-step process will likely find that it's a difficult but very rewarding effort.

Profiling: Where Are You Now?

The first step, profiling, not only confirms what is generally known about the market but also adds insight regarding where we have had success, in a more quantitative manner. Once the profiling analysis has been completed, it can be used as one of the inputs to target future marketing efforts. It also lays the foundation for the quantification of sales opportunities and the new sales coverage model.

The anecdotal examples of success almost always come from sales. Too often I hear of a new customer who is in the X industry and find that a major marketing and sales initiative was launched to find similar customers, without any other form of analysis being conducted. On the other hand, most companies have a strong sense of not only what markets are good targets but also where their success has been achieved. However, in almost all cases in which the "insight" on markets exists, it has not been well detailed and quantified. This is typical for a sales-driven company. For many years, marketing communication's (frequently called marcom) job was to create advertisements, develop brochures, build trade show booths, and perform similar duties. Its mission was not to define, for the sales group, anything about the customer base and where sales calls should be directed. This was the job of product and sales management, and frequently, the determination of who were the potential customers was left to the salesperson covering the territory.

My first real experience with profiling was back in the late 1970s when I served as VP of marketing for Samuel Bingham Company in Chicago. If you're in the printing industry, Bingham may be familiar to you, as the company was the inventor and largest manufacturer of rubber-covered printing rollers. We also sold rubber or urethane rollers to other industries such as steel mills and paper plants, but printing was the main market. The sales coverage was driven by two regional managers who directed twenty sales districts and more than one hundred salespeople. Who the salespeople called on was their choice, so long as they met their quotas. Meanwhile, we had several new products to push and were having difficulty getting the sales group's attention—sound familiar? One new product met several unique needs of sheet-fed printers, so we wanted to concentrate effort on this large subsegment of the printing industry.

As a former salesperson morphed into a "marketing guy," I understood the sales group's resistance and needed to find some argument to convince them that it would be worth their time to concentrate on sheet-fed printers. During that effort, I discovered that there were actually lists of printers you could buy—yes, believe it or not, I didn't know that this type of resource was even available. Fortunately, A. W. Lewis Company published a directory of printers that included detailed information about each company. I went to New York and visited the publisher, feeling like a kid who just found a new baseball glove, and quickly bought the book. In those days, only paper copies were available, as the computers were mainframes and used only for accounting. We hand-matched our current customers against the total listing of sheet-fed printers and determined whom we weren't selling. Then we used that information to drive the sales group to sell this new product in an effort to crack sheet-fed printers that they hadn't been able to sell before. It worked, as the sales group now had something new to talk about and a specific list of potential customers, with names and size of presses as a lead-in to their calls.

It sounds simple by today's standards, but for the late 1970s it was a novel marketing process (at least at Bingham) and an effective linkage of marketing to the sales group. What we did was profile the market and establish which companies were current customers and therefore, by deduction, which were not customers in this market segment, and we used that information to direct proactive sales action. Profiling has now advanced to the stage at which companies are profiling not only current customers but also inquiries and leads to determine which ones are worth following up. There are many uses for the results of profiling, and it is one of the building blocks necessary to execute the new sales coverage model.

Profiling: The Process

Profiling should be a basic marketing process that is performed by all companies. Unfortunately, it is not a basic process yet. My estimate is that fewer than 20 percent of B2B firms have actually profiled their customer and/or prospect base. In fact, recently I was consulting with a very successful software company on its marketing programs and found that this twenty-year-old high-tech company with more than sixteen thousand sales transactions had never profiled its marketplace. Here's how the marketing manager answered the "where do you sell" question: "We sell large Fortune 500 companies and government agencies." That was it; no other detail on the makeup of the market was forthcoming. What the company did know was how its sales transactions broke down by revenue, saying that 80 percent of the business rested in 13 percent of the transactions (that old 80/20 rule again). Management didn't even know how many of the sales came from the same company, since the sales records were by location and were not tied to a corporation or parent company. As a result, the marketing objective was to sell more "large deals," but nobody knew where the "deals" were, because no real market profile had been determined, and therefore the high-tech company was flying blind except to direct the sales organization to "large companies." Needless to say, the company is now engaged in a detailed profiling project to identify the best industry segments. This is typical, as marketing is now playing a more active role in defining the best targets, rather than its being the sole responsibility of the sales and product management group.

So, where do you start the profiling process? First and foremost, the customers need to be profiled, for the obvious reason that past success is almost always a predictor of future success. Then the question arises—on what do we base the profile? In my experience, the basic customer profile matrix is supported by two demographic pillars: the industry type and size of company. While there are other profiling approaches (like sales revenue or some other key characteristic), this basic demographic profiling is a required first step. One of the reasons is that these two data descriptions are also the data ties to outside databases from business compilers such as D&B, InfoUSA, and Experian. We need these data bridges to find companies that match the profile in outside lists. It doesn't do any good to develop a great customer profile and then find that no other data source has this information. You become "marketing-locked" if this happens. Once the demographic profile is established, other more company-relevant profiling approaches are insightful and actionable.

Industry Type

The standard definition of industry type has been the Standard Industrial Classification, or SIC, for the past seventy years. In 2000 this definition became a legacy system, as we are transitioning to the North American Industrial Classification System, or NAICS code. The newer NAICS coding has several major advantages over the old SIC coding:

• It includes the new technology companies that were not specified in the old SIC codes. As an example, Cisco did not have a specific SIC code that described its products and was assigned the famous 99 NEC, or Not Elsewhere Classified, number.

• The new coding system is NAFTA consistent and encompasses both Canadian and Mexican firms. It is also the basis of an initiative by the Department of Commerce to establish a worldwide coding system that, as of this time, is not yet in place.

There are other improvements and revisions to this system of classifying companies. To keep updated on the transition, visit census.gov/pub/epcd /www/naics.html.

Even though the government has officially changed to the new NAICS coding, the industry has not. At this time very few companies that have coded their database with the SIC code have taken the time and expense to re-code to NAICS. Therefore, as market demand has not caught up with capabilities, the transition is not very widespread. Therefore, if you are now considering which coding system to use, my recommendation is the newer NAICS system, even though the data compilers are not pushing this new code today.

Once you understand the coding system and what it provides, several other issues need attention before you proceed. First, how deep into the industry description should you go to define the company type? In the old SIC system, a four-digit level fit most situations, which equates to the six-digit level under the new NAICS codes. The decision, in part, rests on how many customers you are profiling. Many B2B companies sell only hundreds of companies, in which cases going to a six-digit level would be too granular and not provide the insight necessary to identify the best industry concentrations or clusters. Therefore, the number of customers to be profiled can help in determining how deep you go into the NAICS definitions. On the other hand, if you need your customers to be truly defined, in as detailed a description as possible, then the six-digit level is best. This is a decision that needs to be made before a profiling process is undertaken.

In addition, a customer base that is composed of larger companies requires further consideration, since they will most likely have numerous NAICS codes to reflect that they manufacture and sell multiple product lines. Just think of how many NAICS codes IBM or DuPont has that describe the company's business units. On this issue, the site or location of the customer may be a tip-off as to which of these codes should be assigned—but not always. Because this is such an important piece of data, the sad fact is that, in some cases, a manual check may have to be made of the code assigned to the customer. A wrong code assignment will lead to faulty profile analysis. The good news is that companies' NAICS codes don't change or decay over time, so once you've accurately recorded the numbers, you can rely on them. Determining the right NAICS code and assigning it may be a daunting challenge if the customer base numbers in the thousands, but it is worth the effort, as this basic demographic fact will be used over and over again to set marketing strategy and sales direction.

Here's an example of this problem. Recently, we were profiling the customer base of one of our clients, Fairytale Brownies of Chandler, Arizona. (By the way, they make the best-tasting brownies you have ever had!) We sent their customer list to Market Models, a good company for data enhancement and profiling. John Dodd, a very sharp database guy and a good friend of mine, is one of the key executives and knows how to profile B2B lists. We tried hard to send John clean data, but as is normal, we only got a 65 percent match rate. The second-largest segment was SIC code 99 NEC. (Yes, we used the SIC code in this situation, as it was easier to match and reference for this client.) Obviously, we couldn't profile the customer database and provide the needed marketing insight to Fairytale Brownies with this large unidentified group of customers. Much to the consternation of Jack Riedel, one of our young, smart account managers, he was assigned the task of manually looking up these companies and assigning the best SIC code. To make the job a bit easier, we split out only the larger customers from this unidentified group; while this reduced the number, it still left over one hundred to look up. These customers did have an SIC code, but the computer couldn't assign the SIC code for various reasons. Later in this chapter and in Chapter 10, there is a more detailed discussion on the problems with the data-matching process. Of the two basic demographic elements, industry type (SIC or NAICS) and company size, the *type of business the customer or prospect is engaged in* is the most important to base future marketing actions upon. Therefore, it is critical to accurately identify as many as possible and record this information in the database.

Company Size

The next key issue is how to define the size of the companies to be profiled. Most people's criterion for "size" is sales revenue. While that may be the desired definition, it poses several problems. Here's why. Most U.S. companies are private. In fact, only about 10,000 of the more than 10 million companies in the United States are public and are required to file factual information on their sales revenue. This means that 99 percent of all U.S. companies do not report their revenue publicly. Ask yourself, if you worked for a privately held firm, how would someone determine the revenue of your company? If the company were asked for that information in a phone call, who would respond to the question, and would the person even know the answer? Even if your people knew the sales revenue, would they feel free to tell anyone? Of course they wouldn't—it's confidential. That's why the sales revenue reported in public databases is modeled based on some other factor, such as number of employees at the company and nature of the industry. Because D&B is also a credit reporting agency, its estimates on sales revenue are better than those of other B2B data compilers, but still, much of its data is modeled as well. Don't get me wrong: revenue numbers exist in public databases, but they are mostly estimates.

Therefore, to determine the size of the company, the number of employees may be a better gauge. This piece of information is not considered secret and is more commonly known among employees. In public databases, it is usually reported within a range of employee sizes. When developing your own information, it would thus be satisfactory to also use ranges, as exact employee size is not as important as the general size of the company. A typical range breakdown is as follows:

1–4 employees	100–249 employees
5–9 employees	250–999 employees
10–24 employees	1,000–2,499 employees
25–49 employees	2,500–4,999 employees
50–99 employees	5,000+ employees

Unlike the NAICS code, the size of a company often changes from year to year and therefore becomes a data element that needs continual updating. Nevertheless, I prefer using the employee count as the company size criterion, since this question will most likely be answered fairly accurately. While the data compilers do update revenue number and employee size definitions in their databases, the question regarding number of employees is one that we also can ask our customers and prospects and receive a reasonably accurate answer to update our records. The sales, customer service, and telemarketing groups or other types of customer contacts can include this question, and therefore, we don't have to rely on the data compilers for updates.

Another choice on size of company should be made at the outset of the profiling process. While the preceding employee size categories are standard in the industry, it may be wise to combine several categories, so that when a market profile matrix is created, there are fewer cells in the overall grid. Generally, three segments emerge: small (e.g., 1–24), medium (e.g., 25–249), and large (e.g., 250+). The specific size definitions depend on the marketing situation you face and how granular you want this definition to be. By the way, the government's definition of small companies is 100 or fewer employees, so be careful in throwing around these terms, as a "small company" definition for one person may not mean the same thing to another individual. In fact, one of the most important issues in B2B marketing is to have common definitions of terms. You'll read more about that later in Chapter 6.

How to Profile

Profiling is a process that relies on matching your customer or prospect record to public information from data compilers and enhancing your record with the selected information (for example, NAICS code and company size). That may sound easy, but it's not! The problems lie primarily in matching your customer record with the same company record in the public database. In many cases, the way in which your customer or prospect record was input may not match the way in which the same company record is input in the outside database. Since I came from the chemical industry, let's use DuPont as an example. There are multiple ways that DuPont could be listed. Here are a few:

- DuPont
- DuPont & Company
- DuPont de Nemours
- The DuPont Company
- duPont (fill in the name of the division and all the variations)

If your spelling differs from the spelling used in the outside database, the matching process may not find the record, as it doesn't see the basis for the match. Several years ago, I got a call from Cheryl Perkins, who had attended one of my seminars. I use the DuPont example in these sessions, and her company, Chesterton, sells DuPont. So, when she went back to work, she looked DuPont up on Chesterton's large customer database. It had seventy-three different listings for DuPont—an obvious problem if Chesterton wanted to see what its total sales were to this customer.

Among the seventy-three listings were several duplicates of the same plant, in addition to multiple divisions of DuPont.

This does not even take into account the mailing address for a company, which has its own set of problems in addition to the "official" address of the location. Larger companies can have as many as three legal addresses. There is the "front door" address (usually the one that the public databases carry); the billing address, which may be a P.O. box; and even the shipping address, which could be a receiving dock. The last two addresses frequently appear on the customer records, particularly if they come from accounting. As one can see, the possible variations are multiple and will potentially cause the computer matching software program to conclude that the two records are different even though they are actually the same company and location.

Several years ago I worked closely with Frank Wagner, who was president of ESA Direct, a Cleveland-based B2B computer service bureau that has since been absorbed by Lee Marketing Services in Dallas. They saw lots of customer files over the years and developed a list of the six most common data errors that caused non-matches when attempting to combine both company and contact records. As a guide for your quality control on data input procedures, here's what Frank found. They are listed in descending order of frequency.

1. Different address/same company
2. Transposed characters at data entry
3. Different spelling/same person
4. Last name only/no first name
5. Different company spelling
6. No company name

Because of this problem, match rates between customer records and outside databases are usually only in the 60 percent to 70 percent range. That is, even though the information on the company is in the larger public database, the software can't make the match. This difficulty is known, and many computer service bureaus have written special algorithms in an attempt to solve the problem. These programs work better than consumer matching software but still not well enough to get much above the 70 percent matching rate.

So, now that you're aware of the problem, what do you do? Well, first of all, ensure that the addresses of the customers in your database are postal certified by running them through CASS certification. This program verifies that the address you have is the same one the post office has and therefore is used as the "official" address of the site. Once this is complete, run the file through the National Change of Address (NCOA) file to catch those companies who may have moved in the past 12 to 18 months. Any computer service bureau will be able to handle the CASS and NCOA processes. Then, assuming that you are using an outside computer service bureau or database provider to perform the matching and enhancement process, be aware of these matching issues and inquire as to their unique processes and capabilities to deal with this problem. The Resource Directory at the end of this book includes a list of firms that have experience in B2B merge/purge and enhancement processes. When the matched and enhanced list is returned, the next step, as pointed out in the Fairytale Brownies example, may be to manually look up the nonmatched records.

There is another solution for in-house matching, and D&B Marketing Solutions provides that. The company has a desktop software program that contains its database and a system of matching named Market Place Gold. This may be a wise investment in any case, because when new customers or prospects are sold or found, the data enhancement process should be done for each new record. It will be cheaper to do this in-house rather than send these new records to an outside firm, given that the number will be small.

Now let's see how this profiling may look once it's completed. Table 3.1 shows an example of a customer profile matched to the SIC code. This is just a standard table showing how many companies matched specific SIC codes in numeric sequence. The second column shows the percentage of the customer base that these matches represented.

The first-level results, as depicted in Table 3.1, clearly indicated that there were some very good clusters by industry—that is, there were more customers in certain industries than others. In this example, commercial printing, lithographic (81 customers), periodicals (46 customers), and plastic products (32 customers) led the list. If we stopped the data analysis here, then these three industry groups (followed by other high customer count segments) would be the ones to target for future marketing

4-Digit SIC	4-Digit SIC Code Description	Number of Customers	Percent of Customers
0782	Lawn and garden services	15	0.3
1521	Single-family housing construction	14	0.3
1711	Plumbing, heating, air-conditioning	10	0.2
1731	Electrical work	15	0.3
1799	Special trade contractors, not elsewhere classified	8	0.1
2084	Wines, brandy, and brandy spirits	9	0.2
2653	Corrugated and solid fiber boxes	16	0.3
2677	Envelopes	14	0.3
2711	Newspapers	12	0.2
2721	Periodicals	46	0.9
2731	Book publishing	14	0.3
2741	Miscellaneous publishing	21	0.4
2752	Commercial printing, lithographic	81	1.5
2759	Commercial printing, not elsewhere classified	24	0.4
2834	Pharmaceutical preparations	13	0.2
3089	Plastics products, not elsewhere classified	32	0.6
3444	Sheet metalwork	15	0.3
3469	Metal stampings, not elsewhere classified	12	0.2
3471	Plating and polishing	8	0.1
3499	Fabricated metal products, not elsewhere classified	7	0.1

Table 3.1

efforts. This "mirror image" marketing approach is based on a basic marketing tenet. Simply put, past success is a predictor of future success. Therefore, one of the first uses of profiling is to find and then target market segments where past success has been achieved. This assumes that the customer base has been achieved by broad marketing and sales efforts. At times, the customer distribution by industry is skewed based on past programs that have targeted certain markets and therefore higher customer counts appear in these industries. This will obviously affect the analysis. In my experience, though, the customer base is usually spread over a larger number of SIC or NAICS codes than the company realizes, even if they initially targeted certain industries. In the profiles that I've done, there has never been one where an insight hasn't been uncovered as to the composition of the customer base. The primary reason is that in spite of the firm's success, no one really ever performed this type of industry analysis.

Penetration Analysis: The Real Measure of Market Success

So far, the profiling process has been based on the number of customers present in a predefined cell in a matrix. As an internal quantitative comparison of how many customers are in one cell versus another, it is a solid approach. If the number of customers is relatively small (several hundred), then the analysis may well stop here. On the other hand, having many customers in one industry may not provide an accurate picture or the whole story. Think of it this way: If you fish in a pond and catch a bass, a trout, and two catfish, the profile of the catch would be 25 percent each for the bass and trout and 50 percent for the catfish. However, if the pond comprises only 10 percent bass, 10 percent trout, and 80 percent catfish, on balance, you got more of the share of the bass and trout than catfish; in other words, you're a good fisherman. Enough of fish stories.

The point is that the share of the market potential is different if I compare the ones I "caught" only against each other versus against the total market available to be "caught." This is an example of penetration analysis, comparing the customer cells against the total market by the same cell definition and determining a "share" of the total, which is a better measure of market success. The drawback for most B2B marketers is that the total number of customers is frequently not large enough to calculate reasonable percentages (remember the old rule of significant numbers). If there are enough customers in each cell, however, a penetration analysis will provide a much clearer picture of where market success has been greatest.

Let's return to the example, calculate a penetration analysis, and see how the ranking of customers changes (see Table 3.2). In this example, the total number of business in the market was determined by first geographically reducing the market to the territory covered by the company versus using the entire listing of companies in the United States.

You can see that the top three markets, based on penetration analysis, are now lawn and garden services (35 percent); single-family housing construction (15.5 percent); and plumbing, heating, and air conditioning (15.1 percent). This ranking not only changes the order of the top market segments but also will sharpen the marketing focus, as these three top segments are more responsive to the company's products (based on this second-level analysis) than the first customer cluster result.

Fundamental to developing a penetration analysis is defining the total market. Any good database of U.S. companies can be sliced by geography to make the penetration analysis more relevant to the actual customer acquisition effort. Here, however, if the base number for the analysis is too large, the analysis will not have statistical reliability, as the percentages will be too small. Your market situation will chiefly determine whether to try a penetration analysis or not.

One final thought on profiling at this juncture: Most of this description has dealt with customers, and rightly so, as customers have displayed a real behavior—they bought! At times profiling of inquiries or leads may also prove to be helpful, as there may be far more of them than customers, and therefore the statistics would be more reliable. In addition, if the customer base has been obtained over a long period, the inquiries may be more reflective of current market interest and thus provide greater insight. Finally, if you have to select only one data element to profile, my experience shows that the best one is industry type, rather than size, geographic location, or some other demographic element. That is why I chose the preceding industry example. The reason is simple; people identify themselves more closely with the type of company they work in than its size or location. If you ask someone what they do, frequently the answer will be, "I'm in the _____ business or industry." I've never heard anyone say, "I work in small business." The marketing leverage is not only knowing what industries to target, but then selecting the messages and offers appro-

Four-Digit SIC	Four-Digit SIC Code Description	Number of Customers	Percent of Customers	Total Business In Market	Percent Penetration in Market
0782	Lawn and garden services	15	0.3	42	35.0
1521	Single-family housing construction	14	0.3	90	15.5
1711	Plumbing, heating, air-conditioning	10	0.2	66	15.1
1731	Electrical work	15	0.3	140	10.7
1799	Special trade contractors, not elsewhere classified	8	0.1	75	10.6
2084	Wines, brandy, and brandy spirits	9	0.2	88	10.2
2653	Corrugated and solid fiber boxes	16	0.3	165	9.7
2677	Envelopes	14	0.3	168	8.3
2711	Newspapers	12	0.2	141	8.2
2721	Periodicals	46	0.9	573	8.0
2731	Book publishing	14	0.3	188	7.4
2741	Miscellaneous publishing	21	0.4	309	6.8
2752	Commercial printing, lithographic	81	1.5	1209	6.7
2759	Commercial printing, not elsewhere classified	24	0.4	381	6.3
2834	Pharmaceutical preparations	13	0.2	116	6.2
3089	Plastics products, not elsewhere classified	32	0.6	542	5.9
3444	Sheet metalwork	15	0.3	263	5.7
3469	Metal stampings, not elsewhere classified	12	0.2	222	5.4
3471	Plating and polishing	8	0.1	151	5.3
3499	Fabricated metal products, not elsewhere classified	7	0.1	137	5.1

Table 3.2

priate for that business type. People will respond to relevance, and the type of business they work in is highly relevant to them—less so for size of company and location.

Targeting: Where Should You Go?

While targeting comprises fewer pages in this book than the other marketing processes, this activity is nevertheless critical to success. It's a matter of doing the process rather than writing about it, as the B2B marketing environments are so varied that to try to boil them down to a formula would be foolish.

The result of the targeting process is a definition of the target markets that represent the best chances for sales success. There is a fine line between a target that is too large and undefined and one that is too small and granular. I often hear marketers or managers say that they want to pursue "small business" or "the mid-market." These are examples of targets that are too large and will only lead to wasted time and money if not defined further. On the other end of the spectrum are target markets that are too small to actually make up a market of any consequence. For example, I have another client that wanted to target only companies that manufacture railroad cars. For this client, which sells gears, railroad car manufacturers are only a subsegment of a target market. Keeping in mind the product or service being sold, a target market should be large enough to sustain a focused marketing effort and possess several, if not more, subsegments. There is no magic formula for size. When you create a list of target markets, the conclusion that you are shooting at too large or too small a target will be somewhat self-evident. Remember that there is a segmentation process that follows, so targeting is just the first step.

Inputs for Development of Target Markets

There are generally four inputs for the identification of a target market:

• **Results of the profiling.** All of the profiling effort has an immediate use in the targeting process. At minimum, the profile will uncover the industry segments in which success has been achieved. While profiles of customers and/or prospects may be too granular if the six-digit NAICS codes were used, this coding system rolls up to a broader definition of industry through the use of five- or four-digit definitions. In many cases, the results of the profiling are also very useful for segmentation within a target market.

• **Markets of known opportunity.** Most companies focus on target markets in which there is a proven sales opportunity. As a result, customer acquisition efforts are focused in known market opportunities, even though, in my experience, the definition is usually too broad. As an example, I frequently hear that the target is "small businesses" or "mid-market," and if that's the case, the target needs further narrowing. Frequently the definition of a good target is not one that can be easily quantified, and a list of such companies is not easily found. Recently a sales force automation client was targeting mid-market companies that have at least ten salespeople. Mid-market wasn't so hard to pin down by employee size, but finding a list by number of salespeople is impossible. So, one of the first lessons in targeting inputs (other than from the profiling step) is to define targets in a manner that can be tied to outside databases and lists of companies. Otherwise, the definition may sound good but not be actionable.

• **New product introductions.** Most companies have new products or services that they are planning to introduce, and for many of these introductions, new target markets are in the picture. One of the main jobs of product or market management is to define the marketplace and opportunity even before effort is expended on product development. Logically, there should therefore be prior work on target markets for these new initiatives. That's in the ideal world. Unfortunately, far too often the product development is driven out of technology ("we can"), with the hope that a large enough market exists for this product or service. I read a study fifteen or so years ago showing that as much as 50 percent of the sales of a new product were in areas that were not envisioned in product development. My first job at B.F. Goodrich Chemical found me working as a product manager for a product that was developed as a denture adhesive (not successful) and then was sold in large quantities as a thickener for cosmetics (very successful). The moral of the story for marketing is that often the targets for new products turn out to be misguided. By the way, another use of profiling is to identify who is inquiring about a new product or service. It can be very useful to actually test or check the assumptions of the new product development group.

• **Competitive openings.** We all should be focused on our direct competition, and this landscape does change. What is needed is a competitive intelligence-gathering process, which is not the subject of this book but is an effort that will routinely uncover openings based on the activities (or lack thereof) of the competition. For example, the shakeout that occurred after the "dot-com bomb" opened up markets for other companies, as many software providers went bankrupt and their customers were stuck with software that was now a true legacy system. In my experience, not many target markets are defined as a result of openings created by competitive movements, and I suspect that fact is due more to lack of intelligence than to companies' reluctance to wade into a market based on a competitive opportunity. This highlights the importance of including a field on the database regarding the competition found at each prospect and customer. Then you can move quickly when a competitor has gone out of business, is experiencing a quality problem, or cannot supply. The competitive environment and not industry type, in this case, now defines the description of the target market.

There they are—four methods to develop target markets. This process is essential, as it directs much of the following activity. It usually is done at planning time—and it sets the stage for the next chapter, which covers segmentation.

Summary

Of all the marketing processes in B2B, profiling and targeting is one that is frequently overlooked or not done thoroughly enough. Of all the sources of marketing mistakes, the lack of selecting the target markets wisely enough is frequently the root cause. We have an opportunity each year at planning time to either improve this process or continue repeating targeting mistakes.

For companies that have been in business for a number of years and have a number of customers and prospects, the data exist to profile and target in a more scientific manner than to assume that the target markets are the best ones for marketing concentration. True, the majority of the target segments will be the same, but it is the ones that do not log-ically occur to the planning group that will be missed or underappreci-ated. This is particularly true if the current description of the target markets is too broad and/or lies in the hands of the sales group, which thinks geographically.

Ron O'Brian gave me the best advice years ago—put your head in the right position and your body will soon follow. A good targeting process will put the marketing "head" in the right position, and the rest of the job will follow so much more easily.

4

Segmentation for Communications

THE ESSENCE OF this book is that the marketing and sales functions are coming closer together and being integrated to cover the sales territory and achieve the seemingly dichotomous twin goals of "sell more" and "spend less." So, just exactly how do you do this? The fact is that, while expensive and increasingly inefficient, the sales call is still the ultimate method to communicate with high impact. In more popular terms, it's the true one-to-one marketing! If marketing communications is to achieve a measure of success in assuming some of the sales coverage role, there is a need to know much more about the customer and prospect. Knowing more about the company and individual within the company leads to messages with a high degree of relevance and, therefore, impact. No longer will undifferentiated advertising and marketing messages get through the clutter and the time crunch faced by everyone. Simply, the higher the relevance, the more the communication will break through this clutter and register with the targeted decision maker or influencer.

The Critical Role That Segmentation Plays

Salespeople have been making their messages highly relevant for decades as they choose what they do and say based on their current knowledge of the customer and/or prospect. In fact, much of professional sales training is focused to equip them with the skills, both technical and professional, to "size up" the company and individual and proceed accordingly. Therefore, to fully integrate with sales and assist in the coverage of the territory, the marketing group needs to communicate more like the salespeople. The problem is that marketing communications is not face-to-face activity and therefore needs a process to develop and build the basis for the communication; marketers don't have the personal relationship with and on-site knowledge of the companies and individuals. The process of more finely segmenting the market, coupled with recording this information on a database, is the primary method for the marketing group to replicate the sales interface as closely as possible. The term *database marketing* has become popular, and in essence, the process of segmentation, data gathering, and communication using the data gathered is database marketing. Clearly, it's not the same as a sales call and certainly not a replacement, but it's a dramatic improvement over the past methods marketers have used to develop communications to targeted audiences. The capability of using a database of information has enabled marketers to act more like salespeople and come closer to that one-to-one communication.

Segmentation: Three Definitions

The term *segmentation* is tossed around freely and thus has many meanings. For the purposes of this book, here are three definitions:

• **Macrosegmentation:** how the company or marketing group is organized to go to market. The definition by industry or market category is the usual form of macrosegmentation that is found at this level. For example, a software company may select banking as a macrosegment when the customization required in the application is unique to banking and therefore it becomes a focus of attention for the company.

• **Microsegmentation:** clusters of companies within a macrosegment that become the bases for more highly relevant marketing communications. This chapter is all about how to create microsegments. Continuing the previous example, small community banks and large regional banks could be two microsegments within banking.

- **One-to-one segmentation:** in essence, a segment of one. Several years ago Martha Rogers and Don Peppers created the term "one-to-one marketing"—a coup for them, as everyone wants to create their own language. Immediately upon reading their book (*The One to One Future: Building Relationships One Customer at a Time*, Doubleday, 1993), I called Martha, who was still at Bowling Green University in Ohio, and drove down from Cleveland not only to meet her but to congratulate her on a great concept and book. My other purpose was to see how this concept, in her mind, extended into B2B, since the book was about B2C, or consumer marketing. We had a good lunch and have kept in contact over the years. While the phrase "one-to-one marketing" has become standard in the marketing world, I think this concept works best in consumer marketing. Let me explain.

First of all, when salespeople hear the term "one-to-one marketing," they immediately say, "I've been doing that for years—what do you think selling is?" And in fact, they're right—sales is true one-to-one marketing. On the other hand, with an accurate database of information, we as marketers can launch communications to one person via E-mail, telemarketing, and even variable-text laser mail. What we can do versus *what's practical*, though, is another story.

Here's the rub: in consumer marketing a technology solution of sending E-mail may be the only communication the customer gets from a company, as there are thousands, if not millions, of customers per company. Frankly, most consumer marketers never communicated directly with their customers before E-mail. That was left to advertising. So with the advent of E-mail, there was a new and affordable medium to use. We in B2B are not just sending E-mail, but are integrating this form of communications with the sales group. Therefore, one message will not fit all—or even a reasonable number—of customers. The amount of time it would consume to structure marketing communications to all the one-to-one segments would completely overload most B2B marketing groups. This is a case where a wonderful-sounding theory breaks down in execution.

Microsegmentation: Definition and Benefits

Microsegmentation is required to execute the new sales coverage model. The meaning of the term is just what it implies—a further splitting of a market segment into smaller groups or clusters, which then are communicated to in a highly relevant fashion. These microsegments and clusters are composed of companies and/or individuals that have something in common relative to your selling situation. One way to test whether or not a valid cluster has been identified is to visualize all these individuals in the same room; in relation to your product or service, do they have common characteristics or share the same relationship with your company? This approach may sound a bit odd, but as it is explained in this chapter, it will become second nature.

Here's a definition to help:

> Microsegmentation is a process of grouping individuals and/or companies that share common characteristics into clusters that possess a unique relationship to your product or service, selling process, or company.

The benefits to microsegmentation are multiple:

• It reduces the size of the target audience, which likewise lowers the communication budget.

• It creates the opportunity for very relevant messages and offers based on the clustering criteria. The more highly relevant the message, the better chance it has to break through the clutter, connect with the target audience, and drive the desired behavior.

• By focusing on the customer microsegment, it magically causes the discussion to revolve around the customer and, in a surprising result, creates the sought-after "customer-driven marketing" processes that companies frequently talk about but don't actually do!

• Once the microsegmentation process has been completed, it can be used to define the data elements required in the database. (See Chapter 10 for more detail on this issue.)

• Finally, a defined microsegmentation matrix of the market can be used to screen inquiries as they are received to see if they fit the criteria of the best segments and therefore deserve to be more aggressively followed up. (See Chapter 5 for a complete explanation of this use of the microsegmentation process in inquiry screening.)

There are other benefits of this process, but there are some dangers as well:

• Having too many microsegments can create too many projects to effectively manage. Once exposed to the concept, managers can go a bit overboard and want all markets finely segmented, with individualized communications sent to each. While this is technically possible, it's not practical based on the number of projects and associated cost that is required to develop the message, execute, and follow up each microsegment. It's far better to hit a few important clusters well than to try to launch too many efforts with insufficient attention.

• The criteria selected for the subsegmentation may be wrong. One person's view of a market may be flawed to the point of misinterpreting how the market is really structured. Good market research and even profiling should provide the insights to select the criteria that will accurately reflect the market structure. Many segmentation schemes are created based on the "opinion" of one or two individuals. Most of the examples of incorrect segmentation criteria I've seen occurred when the "small business" sector was chosen for microsegmentation. The strong temptation is to use industry type or size as the criterion. Frequently the nominal criteria are really based on other factors such as the economic health of the city or region, the age of the business, or recent movers. The lesson to be learned here is that once selected, the criteria used for segmentation are difficult to alter. So, be sure that the criteria selected really reflect a difference between sets of companies that, when translated into different messages and offers, produces results.

• Many subsegmentation schemes sound great in concept, but efforts to put them into action and record the information on a database make it apparent that the data required to describe the segment are either not widely available or not easy to update. Here's a classic example. Salespeople, at times, want detailed information about a potential customer that gives them a reason to call—such as purchasing history. In the chemical industry, the pounds or gallons of the product purchased would be a great way to segment the market, yet this type of data can't be gleaned from public databases. True, the salespeople can gather this type of information when they call on potential customers, but as marketers, we don't have access to it. Even if we were to telephone all potential customers and obtain their consumption data, the numbers would change quickly over time and could not be updated easily. Therefore, a segmentation scheme based on product consumption doesn't work unless there is a public reporting of the data—a rare find, to be sure.

• Even the best segmentation scheme needs the support of other groups in the organization. In B2B the primary support groups required are sales and product management. If they don't buy in, the scheme will most likely die. Members of the sales group are the eyes and ears of the company, and they need to support any segmentation approach, since they must use the information and knowledge that is derived from a segmentation scheme in their daily sales activities and provide feedback on results. The most common disconnect with a sales group stems from the contrast between their geographic coverage base and a segmentation approach that is industry-based. Individual salespeople may or may not have customers or potentials representing the base industries in their territories, and if they don't, then they really don't care about what marketing feels is important. This leads to a process problem: if the segmentation approach is to be used by the company, the salespeople must record information on the sales force software accurately to provide the needed feedback. If they don't buy into the segmentation definition, they won't record the information, and nothing you can do will change that.

Product management may also express resistance if the segmentation approach is contrary to the traditional view of the marketplace and/or how the company has grown over the years. Don't forget that we are attempting to bring change to the traditional sales and marketing roles, and this "newfangled" thinking may not be embraced readily, particularly if the company has a strong product management focus. Product groups segment the market through the eyes of the product—not the customer. This has led to much tension in organizations, as the trend is clearly to move to a customer-based view of the market rather than a product-based view. Microsegmentation is one of the key mechanisms to alter how a company approaches the market and may be difficult for traditional product people to accept. Therefore, there needs to be support for any customer-based segmentation approach within the company, or it won't work. To effect this movement from a product-based to a consumer-based segmentation approach, there frequently is a need for education—from someone on the outside—on the benefits of this approach. Often when I work with clients in the marketing communications department, I find that they have been preaching this change to others within the organization, all to no effect. The phrase "familiarity breeds contempt" applies here, as most product managers only want to view the world from a product perch. Yet when someone like me arrives on an airplane with a briefcase, the message is credible and can help initiate the culture change. It's also hard to get the product-oriented people to marketing conferences or a seminar, so bringing the knowledge in-house works wonders. Same message, different result.

Microsegmentation Approaches

There are many approaches to develop clusters for marketing communications campaigns, whether the target is a potential or current customer. Any or all of the following approaches may be useful for your marketing and sales situation—that decision is up to you. Select from those that make the most sense, and then build your process and database around the ones chosen.

Demographic Segmentation

The most common way to segment is by demographics. This should be done by every company, as it provides the basic data platform required to do most any type of microsegmentation. Here are the common data elements to consider:

• **Geographic area.** We all know that the zip code describes the geographic location. The disadvantage to using zip codes in B2B is that they represent too small a geographic area, even if you're targeting small businesses. The first three digits of the zip code are called the SCF, or Sectional Center Facility—a post office definition. Thus, the SCF is usually the smallest geographic description that is useful in B2B. This is important to keep in mind when you're selecting lists. Also don't forget that area codes are a form of geographic description as well, even though they are being revised frequently. The Ruf Company in Kansas City has one of the best applications of the geo-demographic segmentation discussed here. The company has an econometric-based model that calculates economic health and activity by geographic areas and can be a predictor of business potential, particularly for small businesses, which are more dependent on the local economy than are larger companies. See the Resource Directory for the company's contact information. The most common use of geo-demographic descriptions of the market is to define sales territories and balance workload and potential.

• **Industry type or SIC/NAICS code.** This demographic description was detailed in the preceding chapter and is the primary building block to understanding and segmenting any B2B market. For any company database that is still SIC-reliant, it is recommended that the new NAICS codes, which replace SIC codes, be appended for all customers and prospects. This may require that a manual lookup be performed in some cases. Any major list compiler, such as D&B, InfoUSA, or Experian, will be glad to provide you with all the details on new NAICS guidelines.

• **Company size.** This also was detailed in the preceding chapter and, following industry type, is the second most important building block in developing an understanding of the marketplace. Unlike the industry NAICS code, this demographic fact does change over time as companies grow, shrink, or merge. As mentioned in Chapter 3, my recommendation is that the number of employees be used as the definition of size, since revenue is a much more closely guarded statistic.

• **Location type.** The type of facility may be an important piece to help define your marketplace. Most companies are single-location firms, but typically, as the size of the company grows, so does the specialization of the site. Here are the most common site definitions for larger companies (in decreasing order of frequency, based on my experience):

  • Headquarters or HQ
  • Plant
  • Research center
  • Retail store location
  • Regional or district sales office

Most of the vendors who supply compiled database information contain these definitions or ones similar. Your decision is to determine if site definitions are important and, if so, record them on the database.

- **Fiscal year.** Most companies are on a calendar fiscal year, and this is certainly true of any private or Sub S corporation, as the IRS requires this. On the other hand, C corporations are allowed to select a fiscal year, and by a rough estimate, about 80 percent are calendar/fiscal. The other 20 percent are spread to the other three quarters, which almost always start on the first day of the calendar quarter, for their fiscal year. Why could this be an important demographic data element? Well, if you're selling a product or service that needs to be in the company's budget, you better communicate to the company before or during its budget cycle, or you will miss the internal biorhythms that occur during planning time. When I was with Quaker Oats, we were on a fiscal year that started July 1. That meant if you wanted to sell me sales training programs, you better start talking to me in the spring. We, all too often, make the assumption that the fall of the year is when companies are in the planning process, so we launch campaigns at that time. By having the fiscal year defined, you can segment your list and communicate to companies based on their proper planning cycle and beat the competition to the budget.

- **Year founded.** In my seminars I included the date of founding as a demographic element to consider, but over the years, it began to seem useless. That is, until I said it was useless once, and a marketing manager from National Pen Company piped up with the comment that it was a key demographic way for the company to segment its potential customer base, as they sold pens to organizations on their one-, five-, and ten-year anniversary dates. So, I continue to list it. Likewise, some people claim that new companies need different products or services from older ones—so if the distinction is applicable to your marketing analysis, use this element.

Relational Demographics Relational demographics are an enhancement to demographic segmentation and are defined as factual information that is related to the sale of your product or service. The most common relational demographic elements are equipment or processes in use by the customer. Incorporating this single piece of information may well completely change the message, offer, and total marketing approach. It can be the most powerful piece of information by virtue of making whatever you do more relevant to the targeted audience. In fact, salespeople have been using this type of information for years without ever calling it by a name. It's just smart selling to adjust the approach and presentation based on information about the company. To make this clear, let's assume that you are selling a plastic material such as polyvinyl chloride, or PVC. Knowing if the target company is an extruder, blow molder, rotational molder, or calender operation would make a great deal of difference in not only what you say but even the type of PVC you offer. Another easy-to-understand example is selling software for sales and marketing applications. Knowing if the target company has outside versus inside salespeople would make a big difference in the opportunity. Recently a client, Square D, was targeting hospitals for an automated energy-monitoring solution, and the age of the hospital became the key relational demographic fact, as hospitals built before 1990 were far better targets than those built after that date, due to the capabilities of the newer-generation equipment.

While there may be numerous relational demographic facts to consider, I recommend the following process: Call or visit one or two of your best salespeople, and ask the following question: What single piece of demographic information would you like to know about a company that would make the most difference in your sales effort? Not only is your sales group your best source of input, but also the fact that you ask for the input can help the integration process.

Several years ago, I served as a consultant to a large chip manufacturer on developing the company's database. We wanted to identify a relational demographic fact to use and brought in a regional manager for the meeting. After some discussion and struggle, a lightbulb went on, and he said, "I know what it would be: what type of processor are they using—16-, 32-, or 64-bit?" That turned out to be just what we wanted, and it took a salesperson to give us the obvious answer. Once he said it, all the marketing people, who had been trying to come up with it for about a week, said, "Yes, that's it." Salespeople are smart!

This relational demographic fact to use for microsegmentation is an untapped opportunity for most companies and can be very powerful in constructing highly relevant communications that cut through the clutter. In addition, don't think that your competitors are not working on segmentation schemes. Just like you, they will add the standard demographic data to their files and be able to segment the market based on the data. But if you go one step further and establish a relational demographic field on the database and populate it, then you have a segmentation scheme that is not easily duplicated. In other words, you may be able to perform "stealth marketing" and outsmart the competition. Granted, the data will have to be obtained on a company-by-company basis, and the task will most likely involve the sales group, but I guarantee that it will be worth every dollar of effort. To start, try for only one relational demographic element and then use it to good effect, and enjoy the results.

Sales Cycle Segmentation

There is a commonly accepted sales cycle in all companies. Here's the traditional one: inquiry generation, lead qualification, proposal/quote, and purchase. This cycle may vary from industry to industry and depend on the nature of the product or service being sold, but it exists. Therefore, one of the most logical forms of microsegmentation is to define where specific prospects or customers sit in the cycle and then communicate to them accordingly. They also know where they are in this sales cycle, and thus the message resonates with them. Following is a generic treatment of a sales cycle, with brief descriptions. These definitions may work for you, but if not, then just add the logical steps or terms that are internally consistent with the sales process that applies. Don't try to create a new type of sales cycle, as this would be resisted by the sales group. All you're trying to do now is define *what is* versus *what should be*. The sales cycle may vary by macrosegments of your marketplace, so different ones may coexist within the same company.

• **Suspect.** Suspects are companies that you have some reason to believe should want or need your product or service. They have not indicated that they are interested yet, but they do have the proper profile of a potential customer. Frequently these suspects are on lists that you order from list compilers, can be found on trade show attendance lists, or are included in directories of companies that are members of an industry association. No matter how or where you find these names, they should be called suspects, not leads. Unfortunately, firms like D&B and InfoUSA refer to these types of lists as "lead lists." This nomenclature does a major disservice to marketers, as none of these lists of uncontacted companies are "leads." They are cold suspects and should be referred to this way. Note that at this stage of the sales cycle, suspects are almost always companies and not individuals.

• **Inquiry.** An inquiry is someone who has figuratively raised his or her hand in response to some form of marketing communication. Inquiries are not yet leads, in that you have no idea at this stage whether or not they have serious interest or can even qualify to buy your product or service. Inquiries arrive from different sources and methods, and no matter how they arrive, until they are qualified as leads, they should be called inquiries. One of the biggest mistakes marketers make is to call an "inquiry" a "lead." There is a significant difference between the two, and this topic is taken up in detail in Chapter 6.

• **Lead.** A lead is an individual who represents a company who can buy your product or service and is seriously interested in doing so. There may be several lead categories, including the always famous "hot lead." Another common lead category is "demo," which is usually a whole step up from someone who has merely expressed an interest and capability to buy. Regardless of how may definitions you feel are required to fit the sales cycle in your company, the lead definitions are critical to the integration of sales and marketing to form the new sales coverage model. This level of definition is the ones where the most conflict has occurred between marketing and sales. Again, much more on this topic is covered in Chapter 6.

• **Proposal/quote.** In most B2B situations, there is a proposal or quote step. This, of course, is where the process of obtaining a new customer is quite active and handled by the sales group. Since this is such a sales-intensive process, it may be important to cease marketing communications during the proposal phase so as not to confuse or disrupt the "close." You can't do that unless it's coded on the database as such; in some cases the record should be flagged so no marketing communications go to this company until the close is achieved by the salesperson.

• **First purchase.** Customers are not just customers; they remain in the sales cycle even though they have purchased. The first customer definition is "first purchase." The reason this category is important is that after someone buys from your company for the first time, you may need to focus more on that customer to help ensure the second purchase. Studies have indicated that in predominantly commodity areas (such as office products) there is little correlation from first purchase to second purchase. The first-time buyers may be trying you out and therefore may not really think of themselves as customers yet. Some companies make the mistake of assuming that their salespeople will readily pick up these new customers and treat them properly. The ironic truth is that this may be the exact time to increase marketing communications to help confirm the decision to buy. Customer satisfaction calls, welcome letters, and the like should be directed at first-time customers to accomplish one goal—ensure the second purchase. The same studies just noted indicate a correlation to repeat and long-term purchase once a customer has bought for the second time.

• **Repeat or good customer.** The repeat—or good—customer is a general definition that distinguishes this group from the new or first-purchase group. Customer marketing is detailed in Chapter 8.

• **Past customer.** Here's a question all marketing and sales departments must answer: When does a customer become a past customer? Is it after some artificial accounting period, such as a year? Or is it when the customer feels disinclined to buy from you again and considers himself or herself a past customer? At IBM one industry group was asked how it defined this category, and the answer was that if a company hadn't bought within an eighteen-month period, it was officially a "past customer." When these same "past customers" were surveyed, the surprising result was that almost 50 percent said they were still customers of IBM. A disconnect, to be sure. If we had begun to communicate to these companies as "past customers," we definitely would have been sending the wrong message.

Defining the "past customer" category may be more important than you think. To exemplify, here's one of my favorite stories. Several years after I left Quaker Oats and had started my agency in Chicago, I learned that one of my Quaker associates, Dick Hardin, had joined a company named Oil Dry. Our companies were housed in the same building on Michigan Avenue, and on the elevator one day, there was Dick, now VP of marketing. We caught up quickly and set a lunch date for the following week. At lunch, we got into some heavy discussions of what each of us was doing, and since Dick was one smart guy and marketer, I was eager to hear about his experiences at Oil Dry. The company sells bentonite clay to facilities to soak up oil from the floor of the plant—not one of the most exciting businesses. After some top-line "branding" discussion, Dick looked up from his soup with a sheepish grin and said, "John, actually the most successful marketing thing I did last year was with our past customers." Since we marketers are always focused on new customers, I was a bit taken aback by the comment. Here's what happened. Soon after joining the company, Dick was asked by the president, his boss, to help find a job for his retired secretary, as she was bored and wanted to return to work after having been gone for almost a year. Dick was stumped as to what she could possibly do, until he landed on the idea of having her call the old customers who were not currently buying. She knew most of them and was happy to be back at work. At the end of six months, when Dick analyzed the results of all his new marketing initiatives, one had far outpaced all the others, and that was the former secretary's calling past customers. The actual sales results spoke volumes. Chapter 8 has more on customer loyalty, but needless to say, past customers can be a source of new business—as all too frequently, when they stop buying, the sales group stops calling.

Behavioral Segmentation

As the saying goes, it's what people do rather than what they think that matters. I'm a direct marketer, and this bit of wisdom is music to my ears, as my fellow marketers and I spend our energy to drive behavior or responses. I know advertising and public relations experts are concerned with creating top-of-the mind awareness and positive brand image, and there is value in that goal. But I want to cause individuals to do something, versus just thinking about doing something. Therefore, to be effective, we have to capture the actual behavior and then respond to it appropriately. For example, a microsegment of individuals representing their companies who have responded for a Web seminar gives us a common characteristic that we then can use as the basis of our next communication, to drive— you guessed it—more behavior. Following are descriptions of some behaviors to capture. In your company and selling model there may well be others, and if so, add them to the list.

• **General inquiries.** At times, advertising and even PR generate general responses or inquiries to the company. While it may be difficult to determine the reasons behind them, there may be gold in these inquiries. They may arrive by phone or on the website, among other channels, and it is important to record the media used for the inquiries.

• **Responses to specific offers.** Most marketing communications today contain a specific offer, so it is pertinent to record not only the inquiry but also the offer to which the individual responded. Hopefully, they remember, and so should you.

• **Trade show stop-buys.** I call this category "stop-buys" because that's exactly what most trade show results are—nothing more than people stopping at the booth and allowing their cards to be taken or badges to be swiped. While there are good leads in these "stop-buys," most people will not even remember the encounter. Just ask yourself how many booths you visited at the last industry trade show you attended and how many you can specifically recall. Not many stand out, I'm sure. Thus, this activity should be a separate category of behavior.

• **Seminar attendees.** Whether it's a Web or traditional seminar, the experience for the individual is quite different from inquiring in response to an offer or stopping at a trade show booth. This category of behavior shows a serious commitment on the individual's part, as time is scarce, and to attend a seminar presupposes a high level of interest in the topic. Obviously, you make it a point to record the date and topic of the seminar for future reference and use in the next communication.

• **Multiple responders.** Individuals who respond multiple times and in a variety of ways may be, by themselves, another important category. Rather than keeping all individual behaviors separate and thereby missing people who have made multiple responses, their actions all should be brought together. This group may, in fact, be the most likely to buy, as they are demonstrating continuing interest.

• **Purchasers.** This list would not be complete without referencing those who purchase and become customers. Since this is a progression that is likely based on prior behaviors, you may gain important insight by making an effort to tie the specific past actions to the action of becoming a customer. For instance, if people who attend a seminar have a high conversion rate to customer, then you have found an invaluable piece of information.

• **Calls to customer service.** Here's a behavior that many marketers miss if they are focused too heavily on the acquisition side. Customer service calls may be just that—calls for assistance. On the other hand, they may represent additional up-sell or cross-sell opportunities, depending on the nature of your product or service. Think about how these calls can be translated into knowledge for future sales efforts or loyalty campaigns.

• **Others.** There may be many other behaviors unique to your company that should be recorded for future reference in communications to those individuals. An example is attendance at company-sponsored events. Someone who played a round of golf or attended a pro tournament as a guest of your company will vividly remember doing so, and therefore, you should remember as well. Square D/Schnieder Electric sponsored a NASCAR race car and held large events at the races. The sponsors invited many people to participate and recorded attendees' names on the company database. Not only did this process identify the customers, distributors, and prospects who participated, but it also set up a series of future communications that, over time, will build stronger relationships. (Ironically, even though they felt NASCAR sponsorship was good, they have pulled out—in part because they couldn't measure the impact of the millions of dollars they had to spend to stay at the track. The desire to measure marketing expenditures is clearly driving many decisions now.)

Competitive Segmentation

All products and services are sold in a competitive environment. That's not new, but what is new is having enough information on a database so that specific campaigns can be targeted to companies that use a specific competitor's product or service. Knowing the "share of customer" and who has the other "share" is dynamite stuff for marketers. In many situations, this information can create a microsegment that can be attacked with sharp messages and offers depending on your company's features, advantages, and benefits (FABs) versus the identified competition. Competition can come in four forms:

1. **Direct competition.** This form of competition tends to be the one on which everybody focuses, as it is the most obvious and

consumes the attention of product management and sales in an effort to beat it. Years ago, Roadway Express, an LTL (less than truckload) freight company, decided to record its direct competitors (such as Yellow Freight) in its database. Knowing a shipper's needs combined with who had the business could form the basis of a strong message to position Roadway against the specific competitor. In the trucking business, since it was very much a commodity sell, the knowledge of who the competition was could be very important when a Teamsters strike occurred. Just think of the marketing and sales initiatives that could be driven from a database with this type of information on it during this period.

2. **Indirect competition.** One of the most difficult forms of competition is the indirect type. It's not a direct-offset product or service, but one that can do the same job in a different way. Changes in technology can be indirect competition, as typesetters have found out. One of the best examples of indirect competition is the advent of the fax and how it shook up Federal Express. The competition was not another air express company, but another way to deliver documents quickly. FedEx even tried to open up fax centers in its shipping offices to compete but eventually closed them all down. Here again, defining your indirect competition and then determining if a prospective or current customer is using this solution may allow for creation of specific messages and offers.

3. **Budget or lack of it.** Many times, the competition to a sale is not the other available solutions but rather the inability of the target company to spend the money now for your product or service. It may be that the company will never be able to spring loose the dollars, but more than likely, making the purchase is a matter of timing. Recording this information can lead to more effective marketing communications.

4. **Status-quo attitude.** "Why should we change?" is a tough form of competition faced by all salespeople. In this situation, your product or service fills a specific need, but assuming it's not a breakthrough, like FedEx, the need is already satisfied to some extent by the potential customer. Yes, your solution is better, but—why change? Knowing that this is the hurdle that must be cleared in order to make a sale is key to future marketing communications.

In summary, defining the competitive set and recording that information in the database provides great opportunity for microsegmentation and subsequent result-producing marketing and sales campaigns.

Analytical Segmentation

While this is not a book on advanced database marketing, a brief mention is in order about the use of analytics to segment the market. Most of this type of segmentation, which is used so frequently in consumer marketing, concerns segmenting customer bases, not prospects. The problem in B2B is that the data needed to adequately support these analytic techniques are poor, and therefore, the results can be inaccurate or misleading. The primary purpose of these analytic techniques is to predict the likely response of a set of customers as opposed to another set. In other words, which segment of the customer database may respond better to a specific offer or message than another group? You can find books on the various methods of analytic segmentation. The discussion in this chapter is limited to the two most relevant methods.

Single- or multiple-regression analysis Actually, there are many forms of statistical analysis, and in his book *The New Direct Marketing* (Business One Irwin, 1990), David Shepard details them all. The most frequently used one in B2B is either single- or multiple-regression analysis. Simply, single-regression analysis is finding how one variable affects another. As an example, you might want to determine how much of the total revenue is derived from each NAICS code based on the customer profile, as in the past, revenue was always reported by customer and not industry type. Multiple regression would then be analyzing the sales revenue by industry type and size of company. Using these two variables to see how they impact total revenue would be multiple-regression analysis. We have all done this type of regression analysis on customers, and if the data is accurate, insight into the variables that define sales results will be uncovered. This might well uncover segments that are better-performing than others, and therefore generate a different definition of segments, or even allow you to rank them differently based on the regression analysis.

What is even more insightful is to extend regression analysis to the inquiry or lead database. Frequently, I'm asked by clients to recommend which of the direct marketing tactics will produce the most cost-efficient result. In the new sales coverage model, there will be many tactics deployed to close a sale. We can easily measure the cost of each tactic used and quickly report cost versus result. But what about the question of which *combinations* of tactics produced the best result? This can be a bit more daunting. Multiple-regression analysis might be able to uncover that, for example, the combination of a web seminar and telephone call has generated the highest conversion rate to sale.

For more on analytics, read David's book or contact SPSS (see the Resource Directory); they have the best software for analytics. Remember that if the data is not sound, no amount of analytic work will produce actionable results. In B2B, our most difficult problem is the accuracy and completeness of the data.

RFM—Recency, Frequency, and Monetary This approach has grown to be an extremely important process in the catalog business and, of course, can be used for business cataloguers as well. It applies only to customers, as an actual sale is necessary to perform the RFM analysis. With this technique, the customer file is ordered by the following categories as described:

- **Recency.** The customers who have bought the most recently at the top of the list, all the way down to customers who bought the longest ago.
- **Frequency.** The customers who have bought the highest number of times at the top, and on down to those who have bought just once.
- **Monetary.** The customers who have bought the largest amount in dollars at the top, down to the lowest-revenue customer.

Then, divide each list into quintiles, and assign a score of 5 to the top fifth, 4 to the next fifth, and so on, until all customers have received three scores. Total the scores for each customer. The ones with the highest totals will likely respond to your next promotion in larger numbers than those with lower scores. Sounds plausible, and in consumer marketing it has been validated many times. The problem in B2B besides the underlying data is that many business models do not fit this simplistic look at the sales relationship. For example, what about customers who are on yearly contacts and release shipments monthly: have they bought once or twelve times? How about distributors, who are, in effect, buying to meet end-user demand? What about sales of capital equipment, in which one sale can be in the millions and will not be repeated for several years or longer?

If this approach fits your business model despite its inherent drawbacks, then use it, as it can be a powerful predictor of future behavior. At IBM we tried to validate RFM by applying the formula to sales numbers from a period of time several years earlier and then looking at the following years' sales, and guess what—it correlated to higher sales for those customers who had the higher RFM scores.

Even though RFM may not be applicable for your business situation, there is one element that you may want to seriously consider when constructing a list of customers or even prospects for the next campaign. The element is recency. The more recent the inquiry or purchase, the more likely you are to get a response or additional purchase. This is the most predictive of the three elements in the RFM formula, so use it.

Need-Based Segmentation

A lot has been written about need-based segmentation, and in theory, it makes great sense. Now if it could only be executed! First, let's distinguish between assumed needs and real ones. In basic sales training, you are supposed to "assume a need" of the potential customer based on what you know about the company and its business. Then, through probing, you determine if that need is real or if other needs are more important. We, as marketers, can do the same thing: assume a need for a certain microsegment, and position and pitch our product or service in relation to that particular need. If that can be defined as need-based segmentation, then fine, go ahead and do it.

On the other hand, many articles on the subject assume that you really know the need and that you segment based on that need. The problem in B2B is that even within the same company, the need of a purchasing agent is quite different from that of the manufacturing managers. It rarely is true that all the decision makers and influencers share the same need in the same priority. In addition, needs can be situational and can change along with management or economic change. For instance, speed to market was a driving need several years ago in the dot-com boom, but that's not the case today. Similarly, what would happen to an organization upon the change in top management from a revenue-growth president to a cost-cutter one? I think you get my point—need-based segmentation is difficult to execute.

Job Functions or Functional Psychographics Segmentation

We market to individuals who play various roles in their respective organizations. An excellent way to market is to think of all the individuals who share the same function as a microsegment. Then, instead of marketing vertically to companies with different individuals and functions, segment horizontally and develop campaigns directed at functional job segments across all companies. The messages to a CFO and to a plant manager about your product or service will therefore be quite different, even though the product or service stays the same.

Customer Segmentation

Why have I saved customer segmentation for last? In part, it's because this form of segmentation is so obvious that it is usually the first type that is done. Who buys what products and in what amounts? How large are the customers? Where are they geographically clustered? All of this is good stuff usually needed for sales analysis and not marketing campaigns. However, there is gold in this analysis for marketers as well, since many new sales opportunities will come from current customers. This may seem to be an odd subject for marketers to think about, as salespeople are calling on the customers, and they should know about new sales opportunities—right? That may well be true for customers that are small companies, but as small companies become larger, it is nearly impossible for salespeople to know all the potential areas for new sales. This is frequently a problem for marketers, as the sales department may well have told them to "stay out of the customer base." At one point, almost 35 percent of the customers at IBM had been suppressed by the sales organization, meaning that sales didn't want the direct marketing group to communicate to specific customers—a common proprietary sales posture.

Ironically, in my role as national campaign manager, in which my main job was "demand generation," most of our campaigns were directed at current customers and not suspects, and we were good at generating new demand. The message today is clear: salespeople cannot know everything about large customers, and marketing campaigns should be directed at this group as well as at suspects, leads, and others.

To sum up briefly, smart microsegmentation is an important element in developing the new sales coverage model. Do it well and the rewards will follow.

Summary

The importance of microsegmentation cannot be overstated. A market segmentation that is too broad will leave you with the capability to launch only general messages that will not break through the high level of clutter—you might as well save your money.

Here's another payoff of microsegmentation. In writing direct marketing copy, you attempt to visualize the person you're writing to and write as though you're speaking to that person. Obviously, the better the microsegmentation, the better you can visualize that person, and therefore more relevant messages and offers can be created. The more relevant the message and offer, the higher the results—guaranteed.

Microsegmentation in B2B takes on even greater significance than in consumer marketing, as the sale can be so much higher in revenue from one segment to another. The range of sales potential from one B2B microsegment to another can be so large as to justify the amount of marketing investment made from one microsegment to another. All too frequently, I see the same amount of money being spent on each potential customer segment without regard to which ones might be the most productive. We just sort of fish for prospects, rather than targeting the best ones and going after them with force.

One of the keys to success in B2B demand generation is the number of times you contact a prospect and the sequence of the media of contact (for example, E-mail, mail, and telephone). This is called "sequence and frequency." As each of these three media is quite different in cost, the question to ask is, how much money should we spend on generating inquiries? With a microsegment matrix, the answer is easy—you can obviously spend more on those segments that will produce the best marketing payoff. This is just another use of microsegmentation.

In essence, by performing microsegmentation, you identify those groups or clusters of potential or current customers who will be the primary source of your success—need I say more?

5

Redesigning the
Inquiry-Generation Process

OVER THE YEARS, B2B marketing communications goals have split into two camps regarding promoting the "brand." One camp defines the brand as the company—for example, IBM, Caterpillar, or HP; the other defines it as the product or service—in this example, computers, tractors, or printers, respectively. Experts agree that truly creating a brand and image (the personality of the brand) in the minds of the target audience is not only expensive but also very difficult. In spite of that barrier, it's not unusual for product managers to think that the name of their product is a brand, and they then direct the creation of advertising, which positions it as such.

When I was at IBM in the mid-1990s, Ogilvy & Mather was the company's ad agency, and it still is today. Clearly, O&M is an agency with a historic perspective on advertising and branding. The agency has a phrase for the impression that the brand has in the marketplace: it's called the "brand footprint," defined as the collective view resulting from the target audience's perception of the company and/or its products and services. At the time, IBM's product group felt the company's AS 400 midrange computer, among other products, was a brand by itself. However, while it was true that most people in the target audience knew the name AS

400, Ogilvy's research established that there were only two real brands at IBM. Of course, the company name—IBM—was one, and to the surprise of many, ThinkPad was the other. Yet, the AS 400 group continued to spend significant advertising money to "build the brand." While it may not have been the wrong thing to do, clearly the advertising mission was not realistic.

It Takes Bundles of Time and Money to Create Brand Awareness

The difficulty of actually building a brand in today's cluttered environment puts the goal far beyond the reach of most B2B companies. I know of no study that calculates the cost to build a brand in B2B, as the size of the target market would be the controlling factor. However, when I was at Quaker Oats, my consumer marketing buddies told me that it took $22 million to introduce a branded product to the market, and that was way back in the late 1970s. No telling how much it costs today in the consumer marketplace with the large increase in both fragmentation and cost of media. Yet, many marketers in both B2B and B2C deceive themselves regarding this goal and continue to spend money on brand or image advertising that would be far better spent on generating inquiries and, of course, sales.

This tendency, in part, explains much of the advertising you see with the visually appealing graphics, a declarative or thought-provoking headline, and generalized body copy. Creative directors at ad agencies enjoy this type of communication, as it allows them to create great-looking ads that hopefully win awards. At the end of the ad, in small or "mice" type, there is usually a call to action, which typically tells you to call an 800 number or visit a website "for more information" or "to find out more." Here's a test: the next time you come across one of these ads, call the 800 number or visit the website and see for yourself to what degree the "back end" meets or, in most cases, fails to meet the advertising message. More on fulfillment and back-end issues later, but this lack of tying together the advertising messages and the "what you get" or "what you see" is a major mistake on the part of many companies today. The reason is that different groups are in charge of the front end and back end, and they don't talk to each other very much.

I don't know precisely how much money is spent on brand and image advertising in B2B, but it's a bundle. Just go to one of the three major business magazines, *Business Week*, *Forbes*, and *Fortune*, and count the number of ads that send a brand or image message and that conclude with weak or nonexistent calls to action. My brief survey shows that between 60 percent and 70 percent of all the ads are brand or awareness and do not have a specific or strong call to action. To prove my point, here's the call to action of several ads from a recent *Business Week*:

- Sprint: "See the power of PCS Vision, and get a special limited-time offer by calling 877-723-8777 or at sprint.com." (Notice there are no details on the offer, so readers don't know to what they are responding.)
- IBM: "For more winning plays, visit ibm.com/e-business."
- Siebel: "To learn more, call 1-800-307-2181 or visit siebel.com/casesstudies"
- PeopleSoft: "Learn more by visiting us at peoplesoft.com/real-time or call 1-888-773-8277."

All of these bland or cute calls to action do tie in to the visual or body copy in some manner, but I wonder just how many quality inquiries came from these ads. The rate card for *Business Week* for a full-page four-color ad is around $98,000 before discounts. To me, that's a lot of money to spend and get inquiries who are responding to bland, cute, or mysterious calls to action. Serious business buyers have more pressing uses of their time than responding to generalities. So, how many interested and qualified responses do you think these ads draw? Not many, I can assure you, if my experience is a guide. During my tenure as national campaign manager at IBM, our group had the responsibility to field all the advertising inquiries for IBM and send the appropriate fulfillment package. The real sales opportunities that came from these ads were always less than 1 percent of all the inquiries—and there weren't many inquiries to start with!

Your ad agency will defend this type of advertising as important in building awareness. The question is, how much money can you afford to build awareness and not sales in a business environment that is looking for measurability, accountability, and results? In these terms, awareness is not a result that can be easily measured, but a mind-set. Responses are the beginning of a result. *Advertising Age* now states that we see or hear between three thousand and five thousand messages a day in both our consumer and business lives. Fighting through this immense clutter is not only difficult but also expensive. And even when they're successful in stopping readers, why do advertisements leave readers wondering why and/or to what they should respond? Instead, the ad should drive a behavior when the iron is hot and at least offer people a reason to respond with a specific and compelling offer.

Here's a classic story to emphasize my point. Several years ago, I was in the office of Carl Marino, who at the time was the publisher of *Industry Week* magazine. While I was there, an urgent call came in from his Eastern regional manager. Carl and I were old friends, so he motioned for me to stay seated while he took the call. I couldn't help overhearing his end of the conversation, and when he hung up, I couldn't resist asking for a bit more detail. Here's the story. A new advertiser, Foster-Miller Engineering, in Waltham, Massachusetts, had placed a full-page ad in the last issue and was disappointed with the results. The company was about to cancel the rest of the schedule, and that alarmed the regional manager and now Carl. The "results" to which the company was referring were the number of calls received, or should we say the lack thereof. I asked to see the ad, and from a "brand" point of view, I thought it was just fine. At the end there was that bland call to action of "for more information," followed by an 800 number. There was no reason for anyone to respond, yet the advertiser was measuring the effectiveness of the placement by the number of calls it got from an ad that was not created to drive response.

The Crux of the Situation

Much advertising is created and placed for brand building but frequently measured on a direct response basis. That is, even though the ad was not written for response, its success is based on how many people respond to it. Remember John Wanamaker's famous quote, "Half the money I spend on advertising is wasted, and the trouble is I don't know which half." In this case, we know that the general brand or image advertising is certainly part of the half that is not working. It's only the rare large company that can justify and afford brand/image-awareness advertising today. For the rest of the world, we need inquiries and sales to be driven from the marketing communications budget. In other words, we need to make our marketing communication dollars work considerably harder today than in the past.

David Ogilvy Said It Best

In his book *Ogilvy on Advertising* (Vintage Books/Random House, 1985), David Ogilvy, at the very beginning, made it clear that advertising that doesn't sell is not good advertising at all. To establish his point, he quoted another famous advertising legend, Rosser Reeves, of the old Ted Bates agency. Here's what Rosser said decades ago:

> I'm not saying that charming, witty, and warm copy won't sell. I'm just saying that I've seen thousands of charming, witty campaigns that didn't. Let's say you are a manufacturer. Your advertising isn't working and your sales are going down. And everything depends on it. Your future depends on it, your family's future depends on it, other people's families depend on it. And you walk in this office and talk to me, and you sit in that chair. Now, what do you want out of me? Fine writing? Do you want masterpieces? Do you want glowing things that can be framed by copywriters? *Or do you want to see the goddamned sales curve stop moving down and start moving up?*

Today, more than ever, you want the latter and not the former—yet, ad agencies continue to convince clients that they need witty, cute, and so forth. In B2B marketing the problem is even more acute, since the start of the sales process, from the company's perspective, is an inquiry and not awareness in the mind of the buyer. Awareness is not bad; it's just that we want a "behavior" to uncover who is interested in our product or service, and in this case, that's an inquiry.

If an Inquiry Is the Destination, Then Planning Is the Road

I've jumped on advertising because it is the most glaring example of wasted money, but other marketing communication tactics such as public relations, trade shows, and direct marketing are also poorly executed, assuming that inquiries should be the goal of the marketing communications. Remember, I'm an old salesperson, and the only thing I really valued from marketing was interested and qualified leads for me to call on and close. The start of this selling process is the inquiries the company receives. Inquiry generation supplants brand awareness as the major goal for marketing communications to achieve and is one of the new fundamentals of B2B sales and marketing.

To get there, an improved planning process is required versus what's typically been done in the past. This new planning process will have three keystones:

- Determining the balance desired between the quantity and quality of inquiries
- Developing offers that generate the type of inquiries desired
- Deploying the proper outbound media to communicate to the target audience

In past planning sessions, selection of the media dominated the discussion. This domination was aided by the fact that separate marketing service firms represented each medium: ad agencies for advertising, PR agencies for public relations, and direct marketing agencies for—you guessed it—direct marketing. Each offered convincing arguments as to why its "medium" was the best choice to achieve the marketing communications goals of the company and, of course, consume the budget. So, rather than putting the tactic or media choice first in planning, let's approach this key step from a different perspective.

Quantity Versus Quality

All inquiries are not equal in value. No one who has actually picked up a pile of raw inquiries and made phone calls to more than just a few of them will argue with that statement. Yet, in the normal campaign plan no mention is made of the balance desired between the two extremes of quantity and quality. On first glance, it is tempting to say that we want only high-quality inquiries, and yet there is no marketing communications manager who will not be deemed a failure if the response rate of a direct mail program falls below 1 percent. That's why everyone strives for a 3, 5, or 10 percent response rate. I've actually done one with a 56 percent response rate where the target audience was very well-defined, the brand was known by all, the message was relevant, and we included a dollar in the mailing package (that old guilt motivator always works). We all know that the higher the response rate—regardless of quality—the more it will appear that a good job is being done by marketing. So, inquiry generation efforts are usually targeted at quantity and not quality. Here are several situations in which quantity can be the right goal:

• New product introductions for which the target audience is not well defined and/or the company needs to communicate to a large segment of the market to establish the product market presence. Here, awareness of the new product may be more important than high-quality inquiries. Creating many inquiries means that the market is better engaged than it would be from the passive behavior that results from just creating awareness.

• A broad-based buying process that involves a number of individuals within a company in the roles of users, decision influencers, and decision makers. In these situations education of the different "buying groups" becomes an overriding goal, and by generating many inquiries, this broader educational effort leads to product/service acceptance and an easier selling process.

• The target market for purchase is not well defined, and a wide net needs to be cast to find the best segments of customers. This often occurs when the target is small businesses. In fact, most businesses in the United States are small! The last U.S. Census Bureau study called *Country Business Patterns* reported that the average size of U.S. business establishments is only 16.1 workers. About 54 percent of all businesses have fewer than five employees. Therefore, when you're attempting to establish the profile of the "best customer," many inquiries are required to ensure a sufficient number to feed the analysis.

The balance between quantity and quality is a rather general goal. The way I hear this expressed is, "We need lots of inquiries to feed the lead funnel" versus "We want only serious buyers to respond." These two statements are on either end of the balance board, and no equivalent numeric expression has been developed. The point is that you are actually dealing with the balance required between quantity and quality of inquiries. This discussion also needs to be had with management before the campaign is launched, so that expectations are managed. The mechanisms for controlling the balance are the offer and the outbound medium used to communicate.

In most situations, though, high quality is more desired even though management perceives that more inquiries are better. An education process is required so that marketing communications managers feel free to go for quality and not quantity. Several compelling justifications support higher quality:

• The resources required to screen and qualify inquiries are not unlimited, so the higher the quality and, conversely, the lower the quantity, the more properly and quickly each inquiry can be handled. Significant savings of money and resources in the lead qualification process will result.

• When the market or product is mature, the quality of the inquiry becomes the only criterion to judge success.

• If the product or service has a high price point (in the hundreds of thousands versus just thousands), tire kickers who can't afford the price will consume too much of the time of the lead qualification and sales staff. Frequently, the price issue is not uncovered until much later in the selling process.

Understand that you have this debate not only with yourself but with product/market managers and senior management as well. This discussion sets the stage for expectations of the results. It also allows for the proper resource allocation and processes to be used when inquiries are received. If high quantity is the goal, inquiry screening and qualification will consume more resources. On the other hand, if the goal is high quality, more attention can be given to each inquiry. Best yet, if response rates are low but the quality is high, then the program will not be summarily judged to be a failure if this expectation is broadly accepted. Again, the two ways to achieve the proper balance between quantity and quality of inquiries are the offers and the media of communication chosen.

Offers Determine Why Most People Respond

There are two reasons businesspeople respond to a marketing communication. The first is that the product or service offered is exactly what they're looking for—it meets an immediate need. These "high-need" responses are obviously good inquiries, assuming that they can qualify to purchase. In fact, it's these individuals who most likely will be the quality leads from general brand advertising efforts, as they are motivated more by their current needs and not the advertisement. These responders will almost always call the 800 number, and therefore, these calls should be carefully handled, since the real leads from general brand advertising will be found in the phone calls and not as much from Web or bingo card responses.

The second reason individuals respond is that, while the product or service is generally interesting, the offer is more interesting, generating a reaction of "I want it"—whatever "it" is. These individuals are frequently at an early stage in the buying process and, while not "hot leads," are seriously interested in taking the next step. Therefore, the specific message to which they are responding is a tip-off of their interest. This leads us to a detailed discussion of developing an offer strategy.

The Offer Is Not the Product or Service

Believe it or not, many business marketers think that the offer is the product, service, or value proposition. This is the "offering" and not the offer as it is defined in direct marketing circles. To obtain responses and convert them to sales, there is no question that the "offering" must be well designed and meet a real market need. This discussion is not about how to develop products or services and position them properly against the market need and competition. Rather, it is about motivating individuals to respond now while you have their attention. In many cases, the offer will appear to be a logical extension of the product or service.

The Role of the Buying Process

Chapter 3 detailed the importance of the buying process in developing B2B marketing and sales campaigns. Another important use for the buying process is to develop the most appropriate offer to move the process forward. For any campaign the target audience and buying process should be identified before an offer is developed. While this sounds logical, far too frequently an offer is selected without these two givens in mind. The worst example of a poor offer is a case in which there is something left over from a sales promotion or other activity and the "boss" says, "Why don't we use the (fill in the blank) as our offer, since we have them in the warehouse." This approach will almost always spell disaster. Here are the three general offer categories to use in the development of a good offer to drive response.

Inquiry Generation or Soft Offers

Most offers are developed for demand or inquiry generation. This makes sense, as the primary role of marketing communications is to drive inquiries into the lead-qualification process. Therefore, it's typical for everyone involved to try to come up with offers that will uncover individuals who are at the beginning of the buying process. The false assumption is that anyone who responds to an inquiry generation offer is at this beginning stage. The fact is that approximately 10 percent or more of those responding are in more advanced stages of the buying process. It's just that they happen to see the marketing communications and respond, since their interest is already high. This issue is dealt with in the next chapter.

Soft offers have two traits in common:

- **Low risk.** This means that if I respond, there is no commitment on my part to do anything more, such as attend a web seminar or hear from a salesperson.

- **High perceived value.** This value can be either personal or business. The value is in the "eyes of the beholder" and not yours. As an example, your new, very expensive brochure may have high value to you but probably not to the responder. The higher the perceived value to the responder, the greater the response.

One of the debates in the area of soft offers regards the inclusion of premiums. A premium in B2B is defined as something for personal use such as a calculator, book, or travel alarm clock. Just go to the many catalogs of sales promotion items and pick your premium from the hundreds available. If the response goal is high quantity, then premiums will certainly work. We found that out in spades at IBM when one of the direct marketing campaigns offered three golf balls to a target audience of CAD/CAM manufacturing engineers. The response rate exceeded 8 percent, and the campaign manager was initially a hero. The response was so great that we had to order more golf balls to meet the demand. Of course, everything started to fall apart when the inside sales group began to follow up and found out that what we had done was to identify a group of golf-playing manufacturing engineers who were not really interested in our hardware/software solution. So, in the end, there were very few leads from a campaign in which the fulfillment cost for the golf balls busted the budget. We should have sold the names to *Golf Magazine* to help pay for it!

Do you or do you not use premiums? Well, it all depends (as do most things in life). One guideline that may help is to ask yourself: Is the premium somehow relevant to the unique selling proposition or benefits of the product or service? If so and you want higher quantity, then use a premium. I'm assuming that the value of the sale and customer is high enough to justify the higher cost of the inquiries and leads that will result. A good example of a premium that can be highly relevant to the product and of high interest to engineers is slide charts. American Slide Chart of Wheaton, Illinois, can customize almost anything technical. Engineers truly enjoy this type of premium, and the best news is that they can't bring themselves to throw it away—so it hangs around for years in their desks. Slide charts also carry valuable information for the engineer, and their use will reinforce the product positioning.

By the way, for soft offers the word "free" still works wonders. You may think it is overused, but all direct marketers know that inserting "free" will bump response rates—guaranteed. So even if the premium is without any cost, say "free slide chart" in bold type and you will always obtain a higher response rate.

A few years ago, we conducted a campaign for a software product called RapidWriter. The major benefit of this product was that it saved time for typists who had to enter the same words or phrases repeatedly—for example, in medical transcription. We used hourglasses as the premium in two ways. First, we bought really cheap hourglasses filled with sand that matched the color of the logo and included them in the outbound direct mail piece to create a package that went "bump in the mail." Second, we offered a brass hourglass for response. Not only did the hourglass fit the benefit of saving time, but we found that the promise of a brass hourglass pulled better than a cheap plastic one in the hand.

This finding underscores the second guideline that I recommend when you're deciding about premiums—test. Tests can be constructed in multiple ways:

- One premium against another
- A premium versus another type of inquiry-generation offer
- The premium in the outbound package versus offering it for response

The expense of the premium and fulfillment cost should be carefully factored into the campaign. Not only does it cost more to include a premium, but the associated higher response rate and lower quality of the inquiries will result in a higher cost per inquiry and lead. If the sale is worth the investment, everybody is happy, but the payoff needs to be sold, as frequently management will question why we're "sending out these books to unqualified inquiries"—or so the critics will crow. The best use of premiums is for inquiry-generation offers. I do not recommend that premiums be used for the next two levels of offers, as they lose their relevance to the buying process.

There are many other and most likely better inquiry-generation offers, and depending on your product or service, one or several of the following may strike just the right chord with your target audience:

- White papers written by a creditable third-party author
- Case histories
- Subscriptions to a newsletter or E-newsletter
- A sample of the product or service—in software this is the free CD
- Brochures and catalogues—make them sound valuable
- Something else "free" (still one of the most powerful words we can use)
- Opportunities to attend a "free" seminar or webinar
- Competitive comparisons or charts/graphs demonstrating benefits

The core question to ask when developing inquiry-generation offers is: what would most interest the target audience and cause someone to act now? Acting now is key to response, since if the direct mail package or E-mail message is not acted upon quickly, there is little chance that the recipient will return to the communication at a later date and respond. That's why all offers should have some form of accelerator. Simply, the offer should carry an expiration date. This is particularly important if you're using a premium or something else that has to be kept in inventory.

Without an expiration date, the offer is open-ended and may have to be kept around for a longer period of time than desired.

Lead Development Offers

Most direct marketers are good at inquiry and closing offers, but frequently fail to deal with the middle steps of the buying process. Over the years I have used the term "lead development" (some companies have called this "lead nurturing") to highlight the important role these offers play in B2B. For many products and services, the steps in the buying process are numerous, and the "inquiry" and "close" are just the beginning and end of the process. So what do you offer someone in between the start and finish? If they are not ready to accept the closing offer (this may not be a purchase but instead an acceptance of a sales call), they won't have any reason to respond further. Assuming that you want to stay engaged in a dialogue with prospects, there need to be additional reasons for them to say "yes" and move forward in their buying process.

Think of it this way. After you have outlined the typical buying process for the targeted segment, ask yourself (and others in the company) what offers will move the prospect from one buying stage to the next. These are the lead development offers. Let's stay with engineers in this example, and assume that we've gotten the inquiries by offering a slide chart on the product or application. The technical specificity of the slide chart should logically interest only those who have some need for the product or are involved in the application. Therefore, a high level of quality inquiries should be present in the total inquiry pool.

So how do we move them to the next step in the buying process? A white paper or technical seminar on the web might be just the right offer to move them forward or at least stay engaged with you. This would be the lead development offer. There are many of these types of offers available, and some creative thinking will do the trick. Over the years, I have termed most of these offers "information of value" offers; what will motivate B2B buyers most is valuable and objective information that will enable them to make better decisions, advance in their career, and even get promoted.

One way to start the brainstorming session on lead development offers is to think about what activities or information a buyer would want as he or she proceeds toward a purchase. Case histories might be very appropriate to convince engineers that they won't have to be pioneers (engineers have a fear of being among the beta, or first, users of any technology). Engineers want proof that the benefits promised from your product or service will actually occur.

Lead development offers will have a higher degree of risk to the responder because they are frequently making a commitment to do something, like attend a web seminar. The perceived value of the offer remains high to them, assuming they are truly interested in the product or service. Something interesting happens at this stage; those who are not really interested will not request the white paper or attend the web seminar. They may well have wanted the slide chart premium or the free something-or-other, but since these new lead development offers are more directly related to the sale, the people who aren't interested in the sale will drop out of the buying process. Thus, lead development offers perform a bit of self-selection. Those who do respond are almost always more seriously interested. They may not be ready to buy now, but they do have a genuine interest and now should be considered a lead even though you may not have actually qualified them (see the next chapter on lead qualification).

A word of warning: just because an inquiry didn't respond to the previous offer doesn't mean that, in the future, that individual or company won't respond. My experience has shown that one of the best lists for demand generation is the "pooled lead" list. That's right, that list of all the old inquiries who did not move forward in the buying process is the second-best list for a direct mail campaign. The best response list, of course, is the customer or house list.

The fact is that, in B2B, individuals represent their *company's* interest; therefore, the inquiry reflects a product or service fit or need, not of the individual, but of the company. In essence, we now have an indication that this company represents a likely prospect for our product or service through the behavior of one of its employees. Compared to either response lists (third-best-responding type of list) and compiled lists (fourth-best-responding list) the pooled inquiry list will be highly responsive for new campaigns. (See Chapter 10 for more information on lists.) Many companies either do not use their inquiry lists again or just throw them out—a big mistake.

One caveat: as the list ages, the accuracy of the contact names will decay quickly over a year or two. Therefore, it is important to record the date the inquiry was received in the database so you can measure the response rate of the subsequent communications against the inquiry date and stop using a list when it becomes unresponsive.

There are two recommendations for improving this response rate. The first is just logical. When using a pooled lead list, include a functional title close to the address information. This will help the individual who handles the mail forward the communication to the proper person if the individual on your list is no longer with the company. This works better in smaller companies than larger ones; in the mailroom for large companies, they really don't care and will toss the mailing if they don't have a slot for this individual. The second recommendation is to first call the company to determine if the individual is both still with the company and occupying the same position. This is an expense that can only be justified if the potential revenue of your sale or relationship is high. In B2B, this is frequently the case—so calling to clean up the list may be very cost-efficient. Remember, this individual, on behalf of his or her company, has expressed an interest. And that is a far better list than any response or compiled list you can rent.

Closing Offers

The classic "closing" offer is, of course, for a sale—or from the buyer's perspective, a purchase. While this can and does occur in B2B, most often the sales group needs to engage in the sales process to close the sale. So, for us marketers, the "closing offer" is normally the request of a sales contact from the prospect, either from an inside or outside sales group. This is usually the "close" for us and I'll deal with it first.

How do we get buyers to "close" by requesting or accepting a sales call? Obviously, the risk is much higher, as this is a real commitment on their part. Although the risk is higher, their desire should also be high, since when people are interested in buying they generally do want to see a salesperson. To incite the acceptance of a sales call, a number of offers can and do work. These are normally centered around either the type of sales call that is promised or the incentive that can be obtained if a subsequent purchase is consummated. A customized sales presentation, demo, situation audit, and case history are all types of offers that the salesperson can deliver that will highlight the importance of the sales presentation. It is important to describe "what you will get" in the sales presentation to motivate B2B buyers today, since seeing a salesperson is not high on their list of things to do. To not "romance" the sales call is similar to saying "for more information" at the end of an ad. Specifics sell, and the more specific you are, the better the response and desire on the part of the buyer.

In addition, something the individual is to receive when the sales presentation takes place will motivate them to "close." Obviously, all the valuable information contained in the sales presentation can and should be important to the buyer, but don't forget that we still sell *people*, not companies. A key thought to always keep in mind is that *companies* have never bought anything—the people in the company buy.

Ron Jacobs, president of the Chicago direct-marketing agency Jacobs and Clevenger (and a longtime friend of mine), told me a story that highlights this point. In a direct-mail package that was intended for a senior management audience, one Johnson & Murphy shoe was enclosed with the tongue-in-cheek phrase, "We wanted to get our foot in your door." The promise was that, upon accepting an appointment, the salesperson would bring the "other" shoe. Actually, the salesperson would call ahead to determine the shoe size of the executive and bring two new shoes while collecting the mailed one. Ron told me that it was the most successful campaign that this company had ever done, even though the cost was also the highest. The issue is that this offer was quite personal and was delivered by the salesperson. Enough said.

If your product or service can be sold through direct marketing without a sales call, then the classic direct-marketing offers will work. The strategy in this case is based on several motivators: discount, limited time, limited quantity, and "something free" or added value. Of all these motivators, the "limited time" and "something free" are frequently the best ones to accelerate purchase; if people really believe that a given offer will expire or that they will get something for nothing, they'll pay attention. No one really believes the "limited quantity" pitch—in the words of Jay Leno when he was the spokesperson for Lay's Potato Chips, "We'll make more." Discounts and added value can work, depending on the discount and/or what you're offering. Just remember that these days we're dealing with a very skeptical audience, and the offers need to be real; otherwise they will not be taken seriously.

Remember that all the offers in the world cannot make up for an inferior or out-of-date product or service solution. I've had several clients who wanted to test direct marketing on products or services that are not selling well to see what can be accomplished with this "new" marketing tactic. Well, if it didn't sell before, it probably won't sell now, no matter how good we are.

Multiple Offers

In most B2B direct marketing efforts there is only one offer. This can be narrow-minded thinking. At times, there may be only one offer that's possible, but before deciding on only one, ask the following questions. "Might some of the targeted group be advanced in their buying process?" and "Do I have an offer that might be appropriate to them?" If the answer is yes to both questions, then consider several offers targeted to different stages in the buying process. Here's a generic example using the classic three stages in the buying process described in this chapter, based on the engineer example.

- **Inquiry.** "Respond now for a slide chart that shows the technical features of _____ product."
- **Lead development.** "Request our informative white paper on _____ written by outside industry experts."
- **Closing.** "Request our on-site technical demonstration of _____ product at a time of your choosing."

Two results will occur. First, the total number of responses will be higher, since there are more offers to interest more individuals. Second, those who are advanced in the buying process will most likely respond to the harder offer, as it reflects their current level of interest and need.

There is one problem with multiple offers; when people are confused, they will not respond. So the offers need to be quite different, and there shouldn't be more than three. Based on this concern, I normally recommend only two offers in any communication. Also, think "wide variation" as you construct these offers. By that I mean that the offers should be quite different from each other. Offering two types of slide charts is not a wide enough variation and won't work. The more varied the offers, the more those thinking about responding will pause to decide which one they want. This is an involvement device—and we know that the more involvement an individual has with your communication, the higher the response rate. So be bold, have fun, and offer widely different opportunities for someone to say "Yes, I want that!"

Finally, you will receive responses that have both or all three offers checked. What do you do? Well, first of all, fulfill all the offers and do it quickly. Second, assume that the hardest offer accepted is where the individual's current interest lies. These people are essentially self-qualifying, and what better indication of their interest is there than for them to have selected several offers?

Summary

There are two parameters to any inquiry or demand generation effort—quantity and quality of the inquiries. The tough part is, what balance to strike for the specific marketing effort? The answer to this planning question will be key to successful campaigns—no matter what the medium of communications. The quality and quantity issues are directly related to each other and are controlled to a great extent by the offers you select. Too many inquiries, and you strain resources to follow up and qualify the best leads. Too few, and you run the risk of campaign failure. The right balance must be struck.

The intersection of the buying process and the offer strategy is the place where you obtain great results. If you do nothing else with all the other information in this book, do this. Outline the buying process for the market segment you've targeted and think of the offers that would move the potential buyer from one stage to the next. Use other people's input, specifically people in product management and sales, and generate a list of all these offers. Consider them to be a storehouse of marketing intelligence, and use them in a way that you can both test and measure the results. Once you find the ones that work, use them again and again until they stop working.

6

High-Yield Lead Qualification

OF ALL THE TERMS in marketing, the one that is by far the most misused
and misunderstood is *leads*. It probably started back thirty or forty years
ago when D&B started to sell business data cards. The company called
these three-by-five-inch data cards "lead cards." What a misnomer, as the
only thing the cards contained was the name and address of business
establishments, plus frequently a name of the president, owner, or site
manager. The misuse even continues today. For example, the ads from
InfoUSA refer to the very same type of data as—you guessed it—"leads."
This type of data isn't even an inquiry, let alone a real lead, but rather a
compiled list of companies that you "suspect" may be interested in buying your product or service. This "suspect" status, of course, assumes that
you have gone through a profiling, targeting, and segmentation process,
as described in Chapters 3 and 4, and can demographically define the
most likely "suspects."

Inquiries Are Not Leads!

To confirm this confusion in terminology for yourself, call several of your
salespeople and, without giving them any clue as to why you're calling, ask

them to give you their definition of a "lead." The salespeople's definitions vary from industry to industry—as well as between younger and older salespeople. For example, the definition of a lead in the office products business will be quite different from one in the machine tool industry. Also, my experience is that even within the same sales group, younger salespeople will be looser with the definition, as they are still hungry and will want to call on most everybody. Older and possibly wiser salespeople will tend to define the lead as more qualified and ready to buy than the younger salesperson.

You're not finished yet. Now try this experiment in the corporate office. Ask two or three people in different functions, like product management, marketing communications, and even senior management, to define a lead. What you will probably find is that no two people define the term with any consistency. This lack of agreement, in fact, is one of the major reasons marketing communications people have such a hard time with salespeople. A "lead" to a marketing communications person will be far closer to that of an inquiry, compared with how a salesperson sees it. So, what's the point? Simple. You must have a common definition of a lead that everyone in the company accepts. It's not easy, but it's well worth the effort. In fact, by defining all the terms used in a robust lead process, you will relieve many of the headaches common to lead programs. To start, here are the classic definitions, as previewed in Chapter 4:

• **Suspect:** a company that possesses the demographic characteristics of a potential customer—that is, one that fits your best customer profile. As a golfer, I'll call this the "sweet spot." Notice, in B2B we almost always target the company first and then the individual, so suspects are usually companies.

• **Inquiry:** an individual (hopefully from a "suspect" company) who has in some manner responded to one or more of your company's marketing communications. All the person has done is "raise his or her hand" based on the communications or offer.

• **Prospect:** an individual who not only has responded but also works for a company that fits your predefined demographic customer criteria.

• **Qualified lead:** an individual or even a selling situation that meets the minimum qualification criteria.

• **Sales opportunity:** a qualified lead *and* one who wants to see a salesperson, plus is in the later stages of the buying process and wants to purchase in the near future.

How you define these terms for your company and industry may well be a bit different from these classic definitions. No matter; the imperative is to clearly define these terms and communicate these definitions, so that when someone mentions a "qualified lead," everyone knows exactly what that means in regard to your sales cycle and/or the potential customer's buying process. Misunderstanding of these terms is at the root of many failed marketing programs, since expectations of results are based on perceptions of what these words mean.

My Best "Inquiry" Story

In the early 1970s, I was in sales for the Chemical Division of Quaker Oats and had an eight-state territory. My title was district manager, but I really was a salesman with one junior salesperson reporting to me. In those days, inquiries came to us on small pieces of paper from our marketing communications department. They were cut from larger bingo card responses that were sent to the company on sheets by magazines that ran our ads. Our marketing communications person at the time was Diane Hamburger, who later went on to greater things at Nalco. She would faithfully cut up these sheets of paper that contained a printout of all the inquiries and place them in envelopes for each district manager. Then, every week or so, she would send them out. When we opened the envelopes, many of these pieces of paper would flutter to the floor much like confetti in a ticker-tape parade. Whenever I got one of these envelopes, I would scoop up all the leads (yes, back then I called them leads) and paste each on a full sheet of white paper and faithfully file the pages in my territory folders. When I traveled, I would pull the inquiry folders for the respective city or state and throw it in the back compartment of my briefcase.

So, off to Pittsburgh I went for a week of calls. On the second day of my trip, one of my appointments canceled, and I went to the folder to see what I could drum up. In there was an inquiry and sample request for a solvent called tetrahydrofuran, or THF. It is used in a number of applications including PVC pipe cement and is slightly more flammable than gasoline. In fact, a year earlier, a THF explosion had occurred in Chicago at a firm called Black Swan, and four people were killed. Obviously, this is a solvent not to be mishandled. I found the address on my map—in Pittsburgh you really needed a map, since the streets look as if someone threw a bowl of spaghetti against the wall and walked away. As I drove closer, my worries began to mount when I realized that the location was an older part of town with homes—not businesses. I pulled up to the place and saw that the address was a garage, which was tilting somewhat to the side. I couldn't back out of there fast enough. This was certainly not a great sales opportunity in my multimillion-dollar sales territory.

Now fast-forward to the following winter and St. Paul, Minnesota. It's twenty-two below zero, and my car is frozen in the Hilton Hotel garage. With nothing really to do except watch daytime television, I again pulled out my "lead" folder and began to make telephone calls. One of them was to a company called IRA in Hibbing, Minnesota. This inquiry and sample request was for Polymeg, a urethane ingredient. The individual on the form was Don Moore, VP of research. We had a long phone conversation that I followed up with a visit to Hibbing, a month later but still in the winter. If you like to gamble, fly to Hibbing in the winter: you may not get back! Don was great. He picked me up at the airport, bought me lunch, and later drove me back to the plane. I can actually remember Don waving good-bye as the small plane took off—it was just like a scene from a movie. Only when I called to see Don that summer did I realize why he had taken all the time with me on our first visit: no sane salesperson goes to Hibbing in the winter, and Don was lonely! The result, in twelve months we had a $250,000 account.

How did I know which inquiry was worth following up? The answer is that I had no clue. I did not recognize either company. That might have been acceptable in the '70s, but it's not a sound process today. Sales time is just too valuable to be cold-calling on inquiries. Just think what might have happened if my car hadn't frozen: DuPont might have got the order, as I most likely wouldn't have ever called Don. By the way, if you're wondering, Polymeg went into a urethane sheet that coated elbows in iron-ore-handling equipment. It outlasted steel by a factor of ten.

Inquiries must be qualified today, before salespeople are engaged, as their time is too valuable and costly. Likewise, prospects don't want to see salespeople early in their buying process. I can't think of any situation in which some form of lead-qualification process shouldn't be developed. As guidance, the following sections outline a step-by-step process for you to consider. Adapt it to your marketing situation, capabilities, and resources.

Inquiry Screening

Inquiry screening is one of the least used methods in the lead-qualifying process, but it has the potential of a big payoff, particularly in cases in which more than a few hundred inquiries are received. In most companies, unfortunately, all inquiries are handled in the same manner, even when information is readily available that would help distinguish certain inquiries from the rest. Putting this information to use allows us to concentrate the most promising inquiries into the prospect category and better allocate our lead-qualification resources. An improved yield of qualified leads will result, and in the end, more sales will be achieved as well. The following sections describe four characteristics that can be used to score inquiries into prospects, based on what we know or can find out before we even talk to the individual who inquired.

Outbound Media That Generated the Inquiry

Inquiries come from several sources. The most common categories are the following:

- Inquiries from PR efforts, such as new product releases and trade press stories on the company or its products/services and executives
- Responses to trade print advertising, banner ads, and, for larger companies, broadcast media advertising
- Trade show inquiries and "stop-buys"
- Responses to direct marketing campaigns, both snail mail and E-mail
- Lists of guests at an event such as a NASCAR race or a pro golf hospitality tent

To know the medium that was deployed to create the inquiry is to also know a little something about the quality of the potential lead. For example, on average, inquiries from PR will be less qualified than those from a well-targeted direct mail campaign. Thus, a rating or weighting can be attached to each inquiry based on the medium that was used in the initial communications. Admittedly, we are dealing with averages and will no doubt miss a good lead, but the benefits outweigh that risk. The general approach is to ask: for every one hundred inquiries that are generated by this medium, how many are likely to be qualified leads? Here's a relative scale (10 being the best), based on my experience, for assessing the number of leads that are likely to be found in the inquiry pool generated from the standard outbound media.

PR on the company: 1
Events: 1
Banner advertising—Web: 2
Brand advertising—print: 3
E-mail sent to purchased lists: 3
Industry trade shows: 2–4 (depending on show attendance and why they came)
Product-specific advertising—print: 3
PR—new product releases: 4
Direct mail: 4–6 (depending on the targeting process)
E-mail to in-house permission list: 6
Telemarketing: 7–8 (cold calls to well-targeted suspects)

I've not listed cold calls by salespeople, even though that "medium" has historically been used to generate inquiries. Clearly, each of these outbound media has different costs per thousand, and I'm not proposing one of these channels over another on a cost-per-inquiry basis. That cost must be calculated before outbound marketing communication decisions are made. All I'm saying is that the quality of the leads generated from these media does vary. Most likely you are currently using some or all of these media now. Just apply this scale to better rank inquiries for allocation of the resources to follow up and qualify. You don't have to do anything more than recognize the clue you are given by knowing the outbound media used.

The Offer Accepted by the Inquirer

In similar fashion, the specific offers to which people respond may be indications of their interest. In the last chapter, we explored the various types of offers to deploy. If you follow the advice provided on offers, you will then be able to judge the relative interest of the inquirer based on the offer that was accepted. There's no question that someone who said yes to an offer for a detailed technical report is likely to be more interested and further along in his or her buying process than someone who wants the brochure. Therefore, the offer accepted is another criterion in weighting an inquiry screening system. Here is a list of offers on another 10-point scale:

No offer: 1 (from PR and brand advertising)
For more information: 2 (see the discussion of this nonoffer in
    Chapter 5)
Soft offer: 3 (so long as it's related to the unique selling proposition
    [USP] or product in some fashion)
Lead development offer: 5
Hard/closing offer: 7–10 (depending on offer)

The offer accepted is a big clue as to the level of interest of the inquiry. As noted, frequently a company will handle all inquiries the same way, regardless of the offer accepted—a mistake, for sure. The offer accepted by the inquirer is another indicator of interest and carries even more weight than the outbound medium you used to generate the inquiry.

The Response Media

The media that people use to inquire can also be a tip-off to their interest. The key is to have several response media from which individuals can choose—for example, a phone call versus Web response versus bingo card (yes, they still have them). One hundred inquiries who call in will always yield more leads than one hundred inquiries who use the Web or bingo cards. Again, here's a 10-point scale to consider:

Bingo card—mail: 1
Bingo card—Web: 2 (electronic equivalents of the paper kind)
Postcard: 2 (from card decks)
Trade show: 3 (from preshow mailings)
Business reply card: 4 (from tip-ins and direct mail pieces)
E-mail: 5 (from driving people to the website)
Telephone call—aided: 7–8: (responding to your marketing
    communications)

Telephone call—unaided: 10 (the person found your number and called)

The response medium is not as indicative of level of interest as the specific offer accepted, but it is more indicative than the outbound medium used. People generally know how long it will take for companies to respond, depending on the media they select to use. If people are truly interested and/or want to buy, then they almost always pick up the phone and call. The Web can be disappointing, as response times from companies vary so much. An inbound call is the best. Don't get confused here: not all inbound calls will be qualified leads. There will just be more leads for every one hundred calls than from any other medium.

A question that pops up here regards the use of 800 numbers. Do they or do they not increase response? In consumer markets I believe they do, but I'm not an expert here and don't have any data to back me up. On the other hand, many B2B clients have told me that an 800 number did not increase responses to marketing communications. I believe them, since they tested it both ways. In B2B individuals who inquire are rarely spending their own money to call and thus are unlikely to be motivated by a free call. They need to solve a business problem. I do believe that 800 numbers are important in customer service situations, but that's another story.

Profile or "Sweet Spot" Fit

Chapter 4 discussed developing the segmentation matrix of your target markets. The first use for this segmentation matrix, as noted, is setting the criteria for list selection to match the target profile. The second application is in the inquiry-screening process, screening inquiries to determine if they meet the target market profile. If the only outbound marketing communication were direct mail, sent to a well-targeted list based on the segmentation matrix, then the responses would all fit the criteria—right? Not always! Lists are not as accurate as we would like to think. If a compiled list of businesses is used, the chances are relatively good that the responses would meet the profile, because the list is usually based on demographic criteria that then become the "selects" for compiled lists. On the other hand, if a response list is rented for the direct mail campaign, more of the inquiries will not meet the profile, since these demographic criteria are not often available in the "selects" for response lists. Of course, there will most likely be other inquiries generated from broad-based media, such as advertising, trade shows, and PR. Given this set of circumstances, you should first attempt to determine if the inquiry is from a company that can and should buy your product or service, based on your predetermined target profile or "sweet spot."

How do you make this preliminary determination without calling the company? There are two methods that work. The easier method is to ask several qualifying questions on the response form. No one really minds providing the answers to "What does your company do?" and "How many people work at the company?" These two questions reflect the targeting criteria that you need to determine if the inquiry meets the demographic criteria. When the "what does your company do" question is answered, a lookup process is then needed to determine the SIC or NAICS code. A directory of these industry codes is published by the Department of Commerce, but a better source is frequently a compiled list provider such as D&B, InfoUSA, or Experian, and their online resource directories. This is a very handy resource for business marketers.

But what about all those inquiries that either did not answer the questions or came from other media, in which these questions couldn't be asked? In these situations a more automated process is demanded. For this process, a software product called MarketPlace Gold from D&B Marketing Solutions can do the job, as mentioned in Chapter 3. The procedure is straightforward. Import the inquiries into the software, and have the inquiry records enhanced with industry code and size criteria. The resulting list of matches can then be sorted into those inquiries who fit the target profile and those who don't. The drawback is that not all inquiries will be enhanced. In my experience, a match rate of only 65 percent to 75 percent can realistically be obtained with this or any other software in B2B. The primary reason is that some inquiry records do not match the respective company records in the outside database closely enough, and therefore the software cannot determine that the records "match." In most cases, unless the inquiry is a small firm, the company is actually in the master database, but the software can't match enough of the data fields to establish whether it's the same company or not. Here again, a manual lookup procedure is required to find the match and enhance the record.

To better understand why this match rate is so difficult to perfect in B2B, see the detailed discussion in Chapter 10.

Those, then, are the four sources of clues that you can tap *before* even talking to the inquiry. Not all will be available in each marketing campaign, but when they are, use them. Remember that all you're trying to do is concentrate the inquiries into a richer prospect pool for lead qualification.

If you're thinking about developing a scoring model, here's the weighting that I feel makes the most sense:

Clue	Weight
Outbound media that generated the inquiry	1
Offer accepted by the inquirer	3
Media used to respond (assuming a choice)	2
Hitting the "sweet spot"	5

Clearly, someone who was sent a direct mail piece, called for a demo of the product or service, and is within your best targeted audience has much more potential than an advertising-generated inquiry who responded "for more information," sent in a bingo card, and is outside of the "sweet spot."

No company has unlimited resources to perform lead qualification, and that means that the first job is to concentrate the best potential inquiries for the lead-qualification system into a smaller pool of prospects. The good news is that you just have to use the current information. Admittedly, we're playing the percentages, but keep this twist of a well-known truism in mind: "Inquiries are not all created equal." With the screening process suggested here, we don't even have to talk to an inquiry to place bets on which ones will lead to the most sales. You have the information in your hands now—just use it smartly.

There's Great Opportunity for Improvement

Over the last ten years, Performark in Minneapolis, Minnesota, has conducted two studies on response management, as that's what they do, and by the way, do very well. Their study in 1994 entitled *The Current State of Inquiry Management* was an eye-opener. The study was based on the results of inquiring over fifteen thousand times to advertisements in more than two hundred industrial trade magazines over a five-year period. Most of the inquiries were initiated via the famous bingo-card response mechanism. Here are the highlights:

- 45 percent of the responses took over 60 days to fulfill.
- 12 percent took over 120 days to fulfill.
- 22 percent never responded.
- On average, it took 58 days for the inquiry to be fulfilled (this, of course, does not include those companies who didn't even bother to respond).
- Only 13 percent of all inquiries were followed up by a sales contact (telephone or face-to-face).
- On average, it took 89 days between the time the inquiry was sent and the time the sales contact was made.

When people respond to an advertisement via a bingo card, studies have shown that in about three days or seventy-two hours, they forget that they even responded! If it took 58 days for an average response, then how many people would even remember that they had any interest and inquired?

When the Performark study was published in 1994, one of my clients was Pease Industries in Cincinnati, Ohio. They are the largest manufacturer of exterior steel doors for homes and are a very good company. I mentioned this study to their president, Len Cavens, and he quickly said that this was not one of their problems, as the marketing group was "on top of this." Well, I believed Len, but since he had never done any "mystery shopping," I decided to double-check. I sent in a bingo card from one of the industry trade books that referenced an ad from Pease and their line of steel doors. I noted the date and put a copy of the card in their file. As the weeks went by I began to wonder if the card had been mishandled, as no response was forthcoming. I was about to send in another when, believe it or not, 58 days later, I got not one but two catalogs from them, both with a letter signed by Len. The very result that Len said would not happen. Before approaching him, I checked a bit further as to why the slow response and the reason I got two fulfillment packages.

The first result of my investigation floored me. Here's the story. The inquiries were the responsibility of a part-time administrative assistant in the marketing department. When I asked her how she handled advertising inquiries, she informed me that when they arrived she was to hold them until there were thirty or more, as there was a postage savings at that level. I don't remember the postal rules back then, but regardless, the net result was a penny saved and thousands of dollars lost, as I'm sure that anyone interested in Pease doors either lost interest or bought some other door.

That left the mystery of why I got two catalogs. A few more questions and I had my answer. Apparently, at times, she got two types of inquiry summaries from the magazines. The first was the print-out of the inquiry information and the second was a floppy disk from the same publication—this was during the time that magazines were starting to get more electronic. Well, she didn't think anything of it, and entered both lists of inquiries into her computer. You guessed it, the magazine was just sending both formats and they were duplicates. You can imagine what happened when I informed Len about my mystery shopping—things changed, and fast.

Have the interceding years and the greater focus on lead systems changed the company's behavior today? You would think so, but apparently not. In 2001 Performark repeated the study with the appropriate changes for new technology. This time the sample was smaller; 491 companies were contacted, in total over one thousand times, via one of four forms of response media: bingo cards, web reader response cards, toll-free telephone numbers, and direct web inquiries. Here are the shocking results: 60 percent of inquiries were not responded to within 60 days.

The breakdown of the average response time is as follows:

- 69-day average for bingo cards
- 93-day average for web reader response cards
- 55-day average for toll-free numbers
- 49-day average for direct web inquiries
- 50 percent of website inquiries were never answered

While there are more results (visit performark.com to obtain the full study), the shock is that it has actually gotten worse rather than better. Why? The only rationale I can think of is that during the late 1990s the economy was so good and sales were so easy that no one really bothered with the lead system, as it appeared to be working. Well, times have changed. If there's any area in marketing that is ripe for productivity improvement, it's the inquiry to sales or lead system.

Lead Qualification

Whether or not you implement an inquiry-screening system, the most important step in the entire lead system is lead qualification. Without question, there are inquiries that you have lost to competition. In two different studies, both Cahners and Penton have found that between 30 percent and 50 percent of inquiries from trade magazine advertising buy the product or service about which they inquire within twelve to twenty-four months. Compare that finding with the fact that most companies report that only 1 percent to 5 percent of their inquiries translate to sales. Why the big gap? There are many reasons, starting with a nonexistent or poor lead-qualification process.

Inquiries Should Not Be Sent to Sales

I'd like to use some real examples here, but I need to protect the guilty. Approximately 30 to 40 percent of companies still send every inquiry to the sales or distributor groups without any qualification. This occurs for two reasons:

• There is no budget or system currently in place to perform a lead-qualification process, since, historically, this was not part of the marketing system. The job of marketing communications was to create the inquiry, and the job of sales was to follow up and sell—simple enough, but now a very costly mistake. These companies may well feel that lead qualification is now required, but since no expense-related or organizational precedent has been set, it's hard to add this cost to an already strained marketing budget. Frequently, these past practices will lead to push-back from sales, which see the proposed change as a loss of control when told that they won't be receiving all the inquiries anymore.

• The sales group demands that anything that "goes on" in the territory be sent to sales. Salespeople have a strong proprietary feeling when it comes to their territories and customers—I know, because I said the very same thing to my sales manager years ago.

In these companies the following comment is often heard uttered by the marketing communications manager: "We sent the 'leads' to sales, and they disappeared into a black hole." What really happened? First, the salespeople have learned that these "leads" are very poor and, in their words, "not worth the paper they're written on." So, they scan them quickly, pick the ones they recognize or want to call on, and round-file the rest. Marketing's next step is usually to ask for feedback from sales. The sales group won't provide it voluntarily, so the pressure is increased, and if feedback is provided, it is either incomplete or produced without anyone's having even talked to the potential customer. Yes, that's right, on Saturday the salesperson "qualifies" the old leads by just filling out the paperwork and sending it back. Nobody checks with the lead, and salespeople know it.

If they call on the lead, then something else happens. Because the inquiry is frequently at the beginning of the buying process, the sales opportunity to the salesperson is a long way off, and he or she will most likely drop the inquiry and move on to more "live action." Because the marketing department thinks the salesperson is now in contact with the lead, it ceases any further marketing communications. The net result is that the prospect goes on to buy from a competitor and wonders why your company didn't call again. This may sound like fiction, but I can guarantee you that it happens more than you want to know. This remains the major reason the gap exists between what Penton and Cahners report and your results on conversion of inquiries to sales.

The Most Accepted Lead Qualification Criteria

There are four commonly accepted parameters that define a lead. At IBM we ordered these four parameters into a cute word—BANT, an acronym for budget, authority, need, and timing. Unfortunately, arranging the words to form a cute acronym did a minor disservice to the logical order of the buying process. If we approach it logically, the order of the words as they match the normal buying cycle is represented in the following list. Your job is to predefine the definitions of each of these criteria to use in lead qualification.

• **Need.** What needs or conditions should exist before your product or service would be of value to the potential customer? Some of the needs may be obvious and others a bit vague. List as many as possible, and then rank them in order, from the need that would produce the highest probability of a sale to the one that offers the lowest probability.

• **Budget.** How much money must be available or in the potential customer's budget to buy the product or service? If the product costs $125,000, and the company inquiring is a one-person operation, the chances are that this amount will not be readily available.

• **Authority.** Who needs to be involved in the purchase decision? This assessment can be tricky, as the power to make the buying decision can vary from company to company.

• **Timing.** How soon will the buying decision be made? With commodity products, such as office supplies, timing may not even be a question, since the purchasing is continual. For other products or services, the buying time line may be twelve to eighteen months.

At first glance, it may seem easy to define this series of parameters and then determine if the inquiry or prospect meets the criteria and thus moves into the qualified lead category. In real life it's much harder than it appears. Let's keep in mind the goal of lead generation—to qualify as many inquiries as possible, and not lose any sales opportunities. The reality is that a group of one hundred inquiries received will most likely break down as follows:

- 10–20 percent are just curious or unqualified and are unlikely to buy.
- 30–40 percent are at the beginning of their buying process.
- 20–30 percent are actively engaged in evaluation and will buy soon.
- 10–20 percent are close to a buying decision and should be handed off to sales now.

The job of lead qualification is to separate the inquiries or prospects into these logical boxes and treat them accordingly. Notice that only 10 percent to 20 percent of the inquiries are actually ready for or need a sales call. What do you do with the other 50 to 70 percent who are engaged in the buying process but are not ready for a sales call?

Herein lies the biggest mistake I see in lead-qualification programs, and the explanation for the difference between what the Cahners and Penton studies found and typical results. The inquiries are "qualified" and either passed to sales or dropped. In other words, we can't easily handle those that are not ready for sales calls or are unqualified.

Lead Development Is the Key to High-Yield Lead Conversion

If we are to increase our conversion of inquiries to sales, we need to create a new capability that is rarely found in B2B companies. A lead-development system assumes the responsibility of keeping the inquiry alive and moving the individual and/or company along the buying process until such time as the party should see, or requests to see, a salesperson. Some companies have called this process lead nurturing. The need for this system is particularly acute if the sales cycle for the product or service is lengthy and the purchase involves many steps and individuals.

This lead-development system is the responsibility of either the marketing communications department or an inside sales group. The clear assumption is that a face-to-face sales call is not cost-efficient at this junction and that, moreover, the potential customer probably doesn't want to see a salesperson. This is a major change in thinking on the part of sales; in the past, any potential customer was sent to the field for follow-up. In traditional sales organizations that have always had all potential customers sent to them, a lead-development system will face stiff resistance. To address this situation in creating your system, here are several recommendations to consider:

- Benchmark how many inquiries translate into sales now. This may be difficult, as most companies don't know the real number. If you don't have the information, then estimate the conversion rate, and get some agreement among key sales and marketing people. Normal numbers are, believe it or not, 1 to 3 percent. In part, this low rate is due to poor or nonexistent lead-qualification-and-development systems and the feeling that the "leads" are no good. At least you will have a useful starting point.

- Talk to sales, explain what the company wants to do, and obtain input from the group. Salespeople will normally resist at first, but they also recognize that many of the leads they receive aren't followed up or are dropped after one call. Concentrate on the benefits to them that this system will produce. Better leads, more sales, higher commissions, an easier job, and the like, are all things salespeople desire. Listen to their input, since much of what they know can and should form the basis of the new system. In addition, they will know that the system has been created with their contributions and will therefore be much more accepting than they would if it were sprung on them at a sales meeting.

• Test the lead-development system. This is important, as no matter how much you know, the actual process will not be what you started out with. Begin with a sample of inquiries, or a territory in which a salesperson is cooperating. If you have a choice of salespeople to involve in the test, select an opinion leader within the sales group. This person's support and eventual recommendation will be key to acceptance by others in the group. Start small and measure the ROI so a larger program can be justified to management.

• Keep in mind that much of the lead development will be done by telephone, and this medium is controversial. One of our clients even asked if we had another name for telemarketing, as the people with whom we worked were hesitant to present the concept to management for fear of the negative feedback that they expected based solely on the term *telemarketing*. Today the department is called the "sales opportunity development group." There's not a *tele*-word to be heard in the hallways.

• Clearly identify the buying process for each lead-development program, and chart the progress of a lead through the buying process. Agree with sales regarding at what stage of the buying process the lead should be handed off to the group. Doing so has two important benefits. First, members of the sales group will know that if they don't have the lead, it has not yet reached the proper point, and they will be more patient. Second, and more important, when they finally get the developed lead, they will pay more attention to it than they did to prior leads. Don't forget that you need to change years of behavior on the part of sales. This may not be easy. The key will be their knowledge that when they call on the lead, the opportunity for a sale is real. Salespeople will respond to this. Also keep in mind that the buying process, as detailed in Chapter 3, will vary by the product or service and by the market segment.

• Allow sales access to the database of leads that are in the development process. Salespeople should know what's going on in their territories, and they may well have input or other information that will move the lead along. If the data are kept from their view, there will be hard feelings as well as a price to pay, once the lead is sent to the field, in poor follow-up and feedback. They must feel that this is as much their program as it is the marketing department's.

• If you are in a highly competitive market, benchmark the competition to see if they are performing any type of lead development. If they're not, you will have a competitive advantage as a "first mover." On the other hand, if they are performing a lead-development or lead-nurturing effort, they have the competitive advantage. That news will work to motivate management to support this process and will shortcut the justification needed to budget for this added expense. Years ago, I was working with Roadway Express on database marketing, and the acceptance was slow until an article in a sales magazine referenced the fact that Yellow Freight, one of the company's competitors, was charging ahead with a similar system. Boy, was there a change of attitude and support!

Summary

A well-designed and well-thought-out lead-development system is one of the new fundamentals that must be instituted.

The economics of a robust lead system can be difficult to justify to management. Until proved and measured, the system may appear to be only an added expense. Many times, I hear, "If we need a better lead system, then the salespeople must not be doing their job." The hard truth is that this attitude does not reflect the reality today. Not only are calls per day down from four to three, but even customers, let alone potential customers, don't want to see salespeople. There is no greater productivity improvement in B2B than that found in a well-designed lead system. Over the many years, we have spent millions of dollars in inquiry generation and sales organizations. The missing process step is the lead system that bridges the gap between inquiry generation and sales conversion.

7

Sales Conversion

THE LEAD-QUALIFICATION process described in the preceding chapter is one of the most important elements in developing the new sales coverage model. The lead process is badly broken in most companies, and that defect is a root cause of poor sales productivity. As mentioned, obtaining input and agreement from the sales group is key in being able to execute an improved lead process. Unfortunately, your job doesn't stop with handing off the lead to the sales group. One of the overall mandates is to sell more, and marketing people must begin to assume more accountability for results and not just activities. Therefore, working with the sales group extends through the sales-conversion process. Obtaining feedback will therefore be critical to analyzing if the leads that are being handed off do meet the qualification criteria and produce sales results.

Selling the Sales Group

To truly obtain feedback, you need to sell the sales group on the reasons for cooperation. One of the most frequently asked questions I get from marketing people is: how can I get the sales group to provide the requested feedback on what happened to the lead? In fact, I can stand in front of an audience of marketing people and recite, "We sent the leads to the sales group, and they disappeared into a (pause)"; without prodding on my part, almost everyone answers in unison, "black hole." Then someone in that audience will ask, "We spent lots of time and money to electronically automate the feedback system so that all the salespeople have to do is enter the data on the website or their sales software, and they still won't do it—why?"

Well, it all begins with the starting point that marketing people use in designing feedback systems. The start is usually derived from management's wanting result measurements on marketing programs. Marketing can measure activities, but to get to results, they need information from the sales group as to what happened to the lead—a sale or no sale. To obtain this information, feedback forms and systems are developed and worked on within the confines of the home office. At the next sales meeting, someone from the marketing communications group stands up in front of the sales team and presents the new "this-will-be-good-for-you" feedback system. If you've been in sales, you know that the program dies during the bathroom break. The salespeople look at one another with a "can-you-believe-this?" eye and then trash it quickly on the way out the door.

Two mistakes have been made that will ensure that little, if any, feedback will be obtained. First, little or no input was solicited from the sales group. The design of the program makes this fact obvious to the entire sales staff. Second, and more egregious, the benefits of the feedback system flow exclusively to marketing and management. The system primarily satisfies marketing's needs, and that is clear as well. There are no stated or implied benefits to sales, just additional work for sales to do, and they will tell you in no uncertain terms that they already have more important things to do with their time.

If you want to develop a feedback system that will work, the starting point must be figuring out what the benefits are for the sales group. Then and only then can you integrate the needs of marketing. Here are several well-accepted starting points to consider as the benefits to sales:

• The feedback will be used in a way to allow them to make more money! Yes, salespeople are motivated by money. This benefit could be phrased as simply as "better leads equals more sales." The rationale is that the more we know about which leads are good and which are not, the better we can adjust and seek the ones that convert to sales at a higher rate. There are other ways that good feedback can result in helping to achieve better sales results. Find as many benefits as possible that justify the feedback system and the time the sales staff must spend to provide the information requested.

• If better feedback is obtained, the lead-qualification process will improve and yield better information to salespeople when they make the first call on a company. This clearly points to not only more sales but also an easier job. Traditionally, the "lead" has been given to sales without much more information than name, address, and product or service of interest. Better feedback equals an improved understanding of what information is beneficial beyond the basic sales needs.

• With more knowledge, we may well be able to zero in on better educating and preselling the lead so that the number of calls required to close is reduced.

Feedback is not limited to results on leads, even though that is the most common subject. Another area in which sales must cooperate is maintaining the accuracy of the contact information for individuals and descriptions of their functions. At one time or another, almost all companies have made this request: "Please update this customer list (either hard-copy or electronic forms are sent) with the names of the current contacts." If you have sent out this type of message, you know what happens—or, more accurately, what doesn't happen! When prodded, the sales group complains either that this is not their job or that they don't have the time. Sound familiar? And, in fact, they are right. It shouldn't be their job to correct your mailing list. They are too busy and, frankly, cost too much to be asked to perform such a menial task. In addition, many salespeople do not know all the contacts for each customer and don't want to have this lack of knowledge uncovered. If the company uses standard sales software, much of this information is on the record and should be gathered by a data-replication process whenever the salesperson logs into the server. There's no need, then, to ask for an update with a special request. If no networked software exists, then it may be marketing's responsibility to update the list and present it to sales for review.

Another reason that some sales groups and/or individuals do not cooperate is the concern that if the company knows everything about a salesperson's territory and customer base, the person is in jeopardy of losing his or her job and being replaced by an inside tele-sales person. There is some validity to that concern, as this is happening to sales groups throughout the country. You must remember that salespeople live in a world that cannot be fully appreciated from a seat in the home office. Not only are they physically detached from the company and see almost no other staff members on a weekly or monthly basis, but they also talk to other salespeople—within the company and from other companies as well. They develop their own perspective on "what's going on," and it may or may not be based on reality. I know, having spent five years covering several states in the Midwest and experiencing everything that has been previously mentioned.

The message that I'm trying to pound home is that if we are going to work more closely with sales, we have to start from their viewpoint and situation or we won't get very far. We have to integrate with them and not vice versa. To convert more sales, we need to convert the salespeople.

How Marketing Can Help in Sales Conversion

Marketing communications has a role to play when the lead is turned over to sales for follow-up and conversion. First, let's say that the lead is not only qualified but also a real sales opportunity. By proactively obtaining other names of key people in the prospect's decision tree and then directing timed communications to them in conjunction with sale calls, we are providing strong support to the sales effort. Salespeople would like other members of the potential customer's organization to be informed and support the purchase on the part of their company.

A related sales strategy that many salespeople deploy is to find an individual in the targeted company who can be "sold," and equip him or her with all the necessary ammunition to play the role of an internal salesperson for your company. It works when executed well. Based on this selling strategy, if your salesperson could cue you to launch the "in-depth" attack program, the chances increase that the internal advocate will be met with knowledge and acceptance regarding your product or service. In other words, it is a coordinated attack in support of the salesperson. This is not easy to do and may be applicable only to potentially large accounts, but if it can be accomplished, it will provide a boost to sales conversion.

Most salespeople have no other tool than themselves to communicate to an account. Phone calls and personal visits are the only media routinely used. So, how about equipping them with communication programs they can launch to known individuals within the account they are attempting to sell? These can take on various forms. One approach is to make preset direct mail or E-mail communications available. All that is needed is the name and title of the target, and the salesperson can launch the communication with a push (or should I say click) of a button. The communication is then executed either by a fulfillment house or internally.

Another program that has proved to be effective is having prewritten letters in the salesperson's computer that the salesperson can personalize, print, and send. Most salespeople cannot write good letters, but if marketing provides them, the sales staff will gladly use them. In the new sales coverage model, what is really happening is that marketing is doing more sales-type activities, and sales is going to be doing more marketing. I'm not suggesting a role reversal but rather a better integration of these two different functions to the benefit of the company and sales productivity. Your challenge is to find the specific activities that can make a difference in the sales-conversion process to support the sales group.

Distributors, Business Partners, Et Al.

Up until now, I have not said much about distributors, business partners, independent agents, VARs, and the like. The fact is that the new sales coverage model applies not just to companies that sell only direct but also to distributors, and just as strongly. (I'll use the term distributors from this point on to denote all these types of firms.) If you are a distributor, all the same issues and solutions proposed are also valid for your firm. The point of view that I'm now taking is that in the distribution channel to reach the market, distributors play a key role in selling and servicing the market. The following sections discuss how to integrate distributors into the new sales coverage model to convert more sales.

"Push" Marketing Should Decline as "Push/Pull" Increases

One of the traditional ways that companies have used distributors is to find the best ones, educate and train them, and provide generous commissions and support. The distributors, in turn, went forth into their territories or assigned markets and represented their manufacturers to the next channel member and/or end market and sold. Only infrequently did a manufacturer bypass the distributor and directly communicate to the end user (other than through advertising), as this level of contact was the preserve of the distributor. This model was a relatively good one up until the mid-1990s, when the groundswell for database direct marketing began. At the very same time that manufacturers wanted to receive more end-customer information to feed the database, the distributors became more protective of the data, fearing that the manufacturers would cut them out.

In part, this situation was caused by aggressive use of the Internet, allowing end users much better access to the manufacturers and, of course, vice versa. There's even a formal term to denote the "cutting out" of distributors—*disintermediation*! I first heard it applied to the travel industry, where airlines basically tried to cut out the travel agent by selling tickets directly on the Internet. Frankly, disintermediation worked for the airlines, causing concern among distributors that the same thing that happened to travel agents could happen to them. Therefore, a new paranoia grew, in concert with the growth in manufacturers' desire for information about the distributors' customers. In some cases, the manufacturers began to communicate to end users and prospects without even letting the distributors know. This did nothing but confirm their fears and their belief that they had to protect the customer information.

There was some real justification for a manufacturer's wanting more information about what was happening, particularly with leads, in a distributor's territory. It's sad but true that sometimes when distributors had been given leads, they either did not follow them up or sold competitive products. This happened at IBM when leads were passed to business partners who sold Sun, Compaq, and other competitive products. The change that began to brew in the mid-1990s has culminated today in the development of a new push/pull model by most companies with their distributors.

Here is the basic outline of the push/pull model that should be part of the new sales coverage model if it fits your company's market situation:

- Manufacturers educate, train, and motivate the distributors just like before.

- Manufacturers then target end markets through the use of database techniques.
- Direct marketing programs are launched to these markets, inquiries are generated, and leads are qualified by the manufacturers.
- A decision is made regarding to which sales resource the leads will be passed, based on a preset series of business rules.
- The leads are passed to the selected distributor and are accepted by that firm.
- Follow-up is required within an agreed-to number of days.
- The distributor proceeds to call on the lead.
- Feedback is then sent to the manufacturer within the set number of days.

This procedure may seem a bit strict compared with the laissez-faire days of push marketing. However, what is really happening is that manufacturers are now realizing that they can no longer rely on the distributors to achieve ever-increasing sales revenue by using the traditional push strategy and therefore must exert more marketing control.

Much of the traditional distributor model that is appropriate for the new sales coverage model relates to the nature of the relationship between manufacturers and distributors. Following are the most common types of distributor-manufacturer relationship. Remember that the original reason for distributors was to perform a "time" and "place" function. The functional responsibility that distributors now assume has expanded since those days to include total sales coverage, adding value, and servicing.

- The distributor sells only the products of the manufacturer and, in essence, is an extension of the company, even though they are separate corporate entities. The distributing company may even be a franchise of the manufacturer. Usually these distributors have "exclusive" or assigned territories that do not conflict with other distributors used by the manufacturer.

- The distributor is an exclusive representative of the manufacturer, as the distributor does not handle competitive products, but the distributor sells other, noncompetitive products to the same or different customer group(s). These distributors may have "exclusive" territories but also may well be in competition with the company's other distributors.

In metropolitan areas like Chicago it is not uncommon to have multiple distributors representing the manufacturer.

• The distributor handles the manufacturer's product as well as products of direct competitors and also directly competes with other distributors handling the same products.

Obviously, the closer the relationship, the better the push/pull programs will work and the more effective the database and direct marketing can be for both parties. That said, the fact remains that, no matter how close the relationship is today, distributors have a real fear that at some point in the future, the manufacturer will decide to "go direct." Do not underappreciate this fear.

Many changes are occurring in the manufacturer-distributor relationship, and many new programs are being developed. Here are several examples:

• Agreements are being rewritten to include the distributor's responsibility to share feedback with the manufacturer on leads and sales. This clause needs to be within the "primary area of responsibility" section of the agreement due to precedent-setting legal judgments. (I'll not try to be a lawyer, so consult your counsel on distributor law.) This puts teeth in the requirement for distributors to provide the feedback so desperately sought. In return, manufacturers are agreeing to termination clauses and penalties that are more favorable to distributors. It's a two-way street.

• Depending on the closeness of the relationship, sharing of prospect and customer information is more frequent than in past years. If the distributor is concerned that the information may be compromised or misused, then a third party, such as a computer or marketing service firm, may be called on to hold the data.

• Manufacturers are developing and testing direct marketing programs that can either be executed for distributors or given to them as a "turnkey" program. In these cases, distributors are sharing their prospect lists with the manufacturers.

Changing the "push" marketing strategy to "push/pull" is one of the most difficult goals any marketing person can attempt. Great resistance and suspicion will be met today. However, depending on your distribution model, there may be no other choice to achieve your sales revenue objectives.

Two Classic Problems

A short time ago, a client in Phoenix, Arizona, that sells products to the home-building industry wanted to develop a pull-through campaign. I can't name the company, for obvious reasons. First, here's the distribution channel setup:

Manufacturer ———▶ Electrical Distributor ———▶ Electrical Contractor ———▶ Home Builder

The company encountered two classic problems. First, the company was having an increasingly difficult time in "pushing" through the channel all the new products it had developed. Some of them were higher-margin products versus the standard commodity ones for which the company was broadly known. The past marketing strategy was to issue a PR release, develop sales literature, and have the sales force call on the electrical distributors, who, in turn, were to call on the contractors, who got their jobs from the home builders. As one would guess, the newer products were not selling well. The second problem was that in certain geographic markets, coverage was thin because many of the electrical distributors were selling competitive products and would not handle the company's line.

I began to ask a few questions, and it became quickly apparent that the company had no real information on the channel beyond the electrical distributor. In the past, the company had advertised in the appropriate trade magazines to establish brand awareness but had left it to the distributors to engage with the channel. Now, this isn't a small market, as the following statistics for metropolitan Phoenix indicate:

Electrical distributors	112
Electrical contractors	1,542
Home builders	1,612

It was obvious that the company needed a pull-through direct marketing program to create demand, which starts with the home builder and includes the contractors. In this case, the electrical distributors do not have good information on downstream channel members, making the first job the development of a database on the channel. It's not a small task, but it must be done to ensure this company continued success in the marketplace. Needless to say, the company is reallocating budgets and resources to develop a new sales coverage model that includes the integration of not only the sales group but the channel members as well.

Summary

Converting leads to sales is the most important goal of the new coverage model, and it's a team effort among marketing communications, the sales group, and channel members. Unfortunately, in the past, it has not been a team effort but rather a quick passing in the night, as marketing communications threw inquiries over the wall and sales picked up the few that it recognized or wanted to call on and walked away from the rest. This practice can no longer exist if companies want to survive.

The acceptance by sales of its new responsibility to provide feedback to marketing is mandatory for any improvements to be achieved in the integration of sales and marketing. Salespeople want to sell. It's the job of marketing to make it easier for sales to occur.

8

Up-Selling/Cross-Selling and Creating Customer Loyalty

In my experience, two types of customers stop buying. The first type, and the more obvious to all, is long-term customers. They stop buying for a wide variety of reasons, but as previously referenced, 68 percent stop buying because they just don't feel "loved" anymore. We will deal with those situations and what to do about it later in this chapter.

The First Sale Is Just the Start

The second group is first-time customers, also known as the first sale. Now, in B2B the first sale can be quite involved, as in the case of machine tools or a specially compounded plastic material where the sale is a result of much time and energy on the parts of both the seller and buyer and represents a large commitment by both parties. I'm not talking about that type of sale. The one that is the most vulnerable is the product or service that has a relatively low dollar amount and multiple competitors. Examples are office supplies, single-user software, printing, and sales promotion items, among a very broad array of products and services. Here the sale can be a result of a demand-generation campaign, a sales call, or just being in the right place at the right time. Regardless, studies have indicated that while we may feel that the purchase represents a new customer, the customer doesn't feel the same way! From their viewpoint, they are trying you out (that means the product or service and your company) to see if they want to continue to purchase. In these situations, there is no correlation to repeat purchase from this first sale. The decay rate of first-time customers is high, and therefore, much opportunity is lost.

Most companies don't even track first-time customer loss, as the statistics are buried in the overall sales numbers. We recently began working with a company in Phoenix, Arizona, that sells food items for corporate gift giving. Fairytale Brownies is a great story of two childhood friends who remained close and started a company together some years after college, or as Elaine Spiltany puts it—a fairy-tale story. They are growing at more than 35 percent per year and sell to both consumers and businesses through catalogs. Over the ten years in which they have been in business, a large number of business customers have bought in Phoenix (they do make the best brownies on earth), and each year they send a catalog to the mailing list and wait for the phone to ring. This year, in an effort to proactively increase their B2B sales, they hired a salesperson to cover the more than four thousand local customers. Remember, they have been growing at an annual rate of more than 35 percent. When we analyzed the sales revenue by customer, it was a shock to everyone that 31 percent of the largest customers had not repurchased the following year. It's obvious where the new salesperson will be placing her efforts.

The Job Is to Get the Second Sale

The brief story just recounted exemplifies that even companies that have a great product and are growing fast can have an undiscovered large decay rate among first-time buyers. The message is that first-time customers must be converted to second-time customers. The payoff is that there is a high correlation to long-time purchase among customers that have bought a second time. In fact, I've begun proposing that first-time customers be put into a separate group and called "very highly qualified leads," since additional effort is needed to truly convert them to real repeat customers.

Up-Selling

Up-selling is simply selling more products or services to the same customer. For the purpose of definition, these products and/or services are either the same or closely related to each other and do not represent a new category of purchase. For example, I buy most of my office supplies from Staples. Buying more or all of my office supplies from the company would be an up-sell, whereas buying a computer would be a cross-sell, since the rationale that is used to buy office supplies does not easily translate to computers, even though Staples carries both.

As mentioned, when customers first buy from you, they are "trying you out." Then, it is hoped, comes the second sale and repeat sales, so that eventually the customer is purchasing its entire category of requirements from you. This concept is known as "share of customer," a term first proposed by Peppers and Rogers in their groundbreaking book *One-to-One Marketing*. While I give them great credit for coining the term, in B2B this concept has been around ever since salespeople have been calling on customers. If you were a salesperson, it was crystal clear that you went after all the business and weren't satisfied until you got 100 percent or close to it.

When I think back on my days in sales, the up-sell situation that stands out the most occurred at Ford Motor when I was with Quaker Oats Chemical. Here's the story. We sold Ford a solvent that was used in the process of applying the coating to vinyl seat covers—remember those days? When I inherited the territory, we had a contract with Ford for 20 percent of its requirements, which amounted to several hundred thousand dollars each year. Try as hard as I could, John Zerbeck in corporate purchasing would not increase our percentage. DuPont was our only competitor, and it had much deeper ties to Ford than just this one product, so it got 80 percent. There was no way to budge him, and I tried with lunches, frequent calls—all the sales approaches I could think of, as we were not going to lower the price.

Being somewhat young and naive, I also began calling on the plant in Mt. Clemens, Michigan, that used the solvent. Dick Rivard was the production control manager, and he told me quickly that he had no say over the contract and was not concerned with price. His needs were different, in that when his people needed a 5,000-gallon-tank truck shipment, it was frequently because they were running low on solvent (it evaporated fast and could escape the hold tank if there was any type of leak) and the plant might have to shut down. In the automotive industry, a plant shutdown was a major event and not one for which you wanted to be responsible. Both our plant and DuPont's were hundreds of miles away, so it could take up to three days to order, ship, and receive this solvent. After hearing Dick's needs, I contacted a local chemical distributor, Gage Products, in Detroit, and arranged for the company to store our solvent in bulk. We also signed Gage up as our local distributor for small-drum or split-tank truck shipments to other customers. And as I expected, when Dick had a "quick shipment" to order, he called us, since we had solvent not more than fifty miles away and could deliver the same day if required. As the year went on, these "quick shipments" seemed to be coming more frequently. At the end of the year, when we began contract negotiations, the purchasing agent was not happy, as we had actually gotten 60 percent of Ford's requirements. In fact, I found out that the purchasing agent had called Dick at the plant and read him the riot act for ordering more from Quaker than allowed. His response was classic: "If your suppliers can't meet our production schedules, then I'll order from those who can." End of story in the automotive industry.

So, what's the point as it relates to up-selling? First, with salespeople not being able to call on all the decision makers and influencers as frequently, marketing communications must pick up the slack. The first sale is but the pinhole we can invade to sell more, and the new coverage model is envisioned to help the sales group do just that—penetrate the account. In the Ford story, two openings existed that were not attended to by DuPont. First, DuPont's salespeople were not calling on the plant, as they felt secure by having the contract, which stated that DuPont was to get 80 percent of requirements. They were missing developing a relationship with and listening to a key decision influencer. Second, they were not meeting the different needs of the influencer. When we established local storage, in effect, we allowed the decision influencer to become the decision maker.

There is a decision tree in any organization (except the very small ones), and it is mandatory that we find out who the people are that make up this tree and communicate to them based on their needs, which, at times, differ. Getting the sale is one thing; keeping and growing the relationship is quite another. This is a key element in working with sales, as we can be of great assistance in helping penetrate the account with target messages addressing different functional needs. As the salespeople can't see everyone on the decision tree today, marketing communications needs to step up and take on this responsibility in combination with sales. This effort obviously requires a database containing information on these individuals and the functions they perform in the organization.

Cross-Selling Is Harder Than You Think

Up-selling a current account can be relatively easy, but cross-selling is quite another challenge. All too often, I've heard the following statement made by home office types: "Since we already have these customers, let's sell them our other products/services." Everyone looks around the room and smiles at that great gem of wisdom. Something funny happens on the way to the bank, though: nobody told the customers that they should buy another product/service from this company, and they don't. There are as many cross-sell programs on the dead campaign pile as there have been successes. This is a much harder sales and marketing goal to achieve than anticipated. Customers buy a given product or service based on its unique attributes and value proposition, and those qualities are not easily transferred to another category even though the same company is offering it.

The most notable examples of companies failing at cross-selling are the utility firms that were unleashed from regulation in the 1990s. Besides the fact that they weren't good marketers to begin with, they thought that just because a customer bought electricity from them that this same customer would buy security services. It made sense to them, since the same wiring that was used for delivery of electricity services could be used for alarms. The customers didn't agree, as home and office security was the domain of firms like ADT and not the utilities. Almost all of these efforts to cross-sell met with failure.

In Arizona, one of the local utilities is APS, and they fell into this trap in the mid-1990s. They even created a separate division to sell home and office security systems. I met the president of the division on a trip to Phoenix and was bemused to hear that he didn't feel much of a marketing budget was needed in Arizona because they were so well-known. He became concerned when they moved outside of Arizona, as nobody knew them in, say, Colorado. So a hefty marketing and advertising budget was devoted to those non-Arizona markets. Guess what? They did better outside of Arizona, since they'd made their value proposition known to these markets. In their home turf, they tried to trade too much on the brand awareness, assuming that current customers would flock to buy. It didn't work and the division went under. Why? Well, most studies indicated that customers didn't feel the local utility had any more credibility in home security than any other new entry in the market. Since they were new and underfunded in the marketing effort, they went down to defeat.

In the same vein, banks think that just because you have a commercial checking account with them, you feel inclined to give them your lending needs. Yes, both involve money, but one does not equate to the other in commitment and depth of relationship required.

The message to take away is that cross-selling is almost the same as obtaining a new customer. You should approach current customers with the same dedicated effort given to new prospects. We found this to be true at IBM. Almost all of our demand-generation campaigns were directed at current customers. The advantage was that the company had bought from IBM. The assumption that we didn't make was that it would be easy or that the salesperson knew about all the new potential opportunities—they didn't. Selling current customers other products and services is a great objective; just don't underestimate how hard it will be to achieve.

Achieving Customer Loyalty in B2B

Customer loyalty in B2B is the ultimate objective for both the sales and marketing groups, as the payoff in terms of lifetime value is great in both dollar and margin amounts. Frederick Reichheld's book *The Loyalty Effect* is a must-read for anyone who has not already jumped on the loyalty bandwagon. He convincingly lays out the case for the importance of loyalty, which includes higher profit, lower marketing acquisition costs, more referrals, and, of course, lower customer decay rates. All of this applies to B2B, but there's one big difference between selling other businesses and selling consumers: we don't have frequent flyer or discount card programs! In almost all B2B situations, awarding points or allowing discounts for a frequent purchase is not a workable solution. We do have volume discounts, but these are usually negotiated in advance of the sale and are not really ongoing loyalty programs. It's possible for credit cards or other low-priced commodity items, but not for computer hardware, lift trucks, office-cleaning services, and the like. For one thing, it would seem too close to a bribe to have some type of personal frequency program for the wide array of products and services that a business buys. Also, it is generally against company policy (particularly in large firms) to accept gifts or rewards that are in excess of $25 to $50.

I had a close encounter with this limit on gifts at IBM, and the story is rather funny. As national campaign manager, I had responsibility for the direct marketing agencies and their relationship with IBM. At Christmastime, as agencies tend to do, they sent holiday items to their clients. Sitting at my desk one day, I got a FedEx package from Bronner Schlosberg and Humphry (now Digitas), an agency we used that was based in Boston. The package contained a letter and picture of a lobster in a pot. An odd gift, it seemed. Then I read the letter, and it explained that the company's Christmas gift to us at IBM (and all their other clients) would have been a live Maine lobster, but unfortunately the agency didn't know until the last minute that we couldn't accept gifts worth more than $25. The lobster and all the accompanying items were valued at more than that, so, in its place was the next best thing—a picture of the lobster we would have gotten. We all had a good laugh but, in the end, no lobster! Ironically, my loyalty to the agency was based on its work and the personal relationship I had developed with Michael Schlosberg, and the lobster would not have made any difference.

On the other hand, I do think there is a fallacy with consumer loyalty programs that are based on rewards. These programs buy your transaction but not necessarily personal loyalty. As mentioned earlier, loyalty is a human emotion. Josiah Royce at Harvard did the original work on this subject back in 1908. He identified a hierarchy of human loyalty: at the top was loyalty we give to a set of values and principles, in second place was loyalty to groups, and third was loyalty to individuals. Nowhere in his hierarchy were frequent flyer programs! So, how can we use this insight to develop loyalty in B2B? I believe that it plays right into the new sales coverage model.

First, loyalty to values and principles relates to the question "What does your company stand for?" At times, the mission and value proposition of the company sound like so many empty words, but if we can effectively communicate them to customers, we stand a better chance of creating and keeping their loyalty. This also translates to product and service quality, which are actual demonstrations of the company's values and principles. Fast responses to questions or problems serve to generate loyalty. Second, loyalty to groups is applicable to the team of people who concern themselves with servicing customers' needs. This could be the account team in an agency setting or the sales team. The representation that your company is a team of people can play well in establishing a basis for loyalty. And finally, the relevance of the important loyalty that is generated by personal relationships is obvious: salespeople were and still are the masters of this type of loyalty.

Frequency of Personalized Communications Is the Key

The challenge, of course, is, given the reduction in sales contacts, how do we develop loyalty among customers who always seem to be seeking just a lower price? The new sales coverage model meets this challenge, since if we accurately record the names of all the people in the decision tree and the contacts with each of these people, we can launch an ongoing series of communications that are personal and relevant to their interests and needs. The frequency of personalized communications will go a long way to creating loyalty among customers. We still must share our values and principles and familiarize them with the team, but unless we communicate the values and principles effectively to all concerned, we will not be able to generate the type of loyalty that comes with a high level of face-to-face sales contact.

Random Acts of Kindness

One of the most interesting and effective ways to engender customer loyalty with key individuals is to perform what I like to call random acts of kindness. First, select your top customers and the key people within each organization—say, one hundred people in all. Then, for no particular reason—meaning in recognition of no holiday or other event—send them a nice gift (below $25) and say, "Thanks for your business. We enjoy having you as our customer." Do not ask for anything in return. I've sent customers the great brownies made by Fairytale Brownies. Do this, and then stand back and be surprised at the response. You'll get calls and letters of appreciation that will be of value in excess of any cost expended. Frequently in business we fail to factor in the human, and this kind of effort can really reach out and touch people.

The Intersection of Customer Satisfaction and Loyalty

Finally, a few thoughts on the intersection of customer satisfaction and loyalty. There is a widely held belief that a customer who is "satisfied" must therefore be loyal. This is a dangerous assumption to make. Here are some facts to consider. In a typical customer-satisfaction survey, customers are given a five-level scale to rate their degree of satisfaction. Here are the standard levels along with typical percentages of respondents:

1	Very unsatisfied	5 percent of customers	5 points
2	Not satisfied	15 percent of customers	30 points
3	Satisfied	45 percent of customers	135 points
4	Well satisfied	25 percent of customers	100 points
5	Very highly satisfied	10 percent of customers	50 points
		Total	320 points

The average score in this example is 3.2. Based on that number, we would conclude that our customers are "satisfied," and we would work hard to improve the average. However, using averages from customer-satisfaction ratings masks a potential problem relating to the decay of specific customers. In the preceding example, one hundred customers were surveyed. Therefore, twenty are either very unsatisfied or not satisfied and represent a real potential customer loss. But which twenty? The average won't tell you. Even more important, the customers who say they are either satisfied or well satisfied are in what is called the "zone of defection." Evidence has shown that these customers, while claiming satisfaction, can be sold by a competitor if they are offered a better deal—whatever that means in your market. In essence, then, ninety of the one hundred customers are at risk. The remaining ten customers are advocates and are loyal and are also a source of referrals.

Your job, of course, is to move as many customers up the ladder as possible, but by having only averages, you don't know which customer is in which level of "satisfaction." In the new sales coverage model, the database record on each customer should contain the actual score or level of satisfaction. Armed with this information, you can treat customers according to where they are in terms of their level of satisfaction. This means that customer-satisfaction surveys cannot be blind and must reveal what customers are feeling. Getting customers to say what they are really feeling may be difficult, but determining where each customer is on the satisfaction scale is the only way to improve loyalty on an individual basis. Having overall scores improve is encouraging, but that will be of little help in stemming the tide of customer decay.

Summary

Up-selling is an important goal of any selling model and must be attacked by everyone involved in customer acquisition and retention. Cross-selling is far more difficult to achieve than first envisioned. Remember, when you attempt cross-selling, that all customers should be viewed as prospects; don't assume that they will buy new products or services just because they buy something else from your company. Creating customer loyalty is key to survival today, as customer decay rates are most likely higher than assumed. A benchmark should be taken on decay rates, and targeted effort should be expended to improve them using frequency of relevant and personalized communications.

9

Campaign Planning and Execution

CAMPAIGN PLANNING NEEDS to change. Until the last several years, when marketing communications planned campaigns, there were three underlying processes and perspectives that are no longer valid:

• The "campaign" was really an "event," as the time period it spanned was generally short (for example, three months) and certainly no longer than the fiscal year of the company. The marketing activities lived within the artificial accounting periods of the company and had no direct relationship to either the normal sales cycle of the product or service being sold or the customers' buying process. In essence, these tactical campaigns were frequently disconnected from the natural biorhythms of the marketplace.

• Second, campaign executions were primarily composed of PR announcements, advertising in trade journals, sales collateral production, trade show promotions, and, most recently, page additions to the website. Little direct mail and telemarketing were deployed.

• Finally, campaigns were not integrated with the sales group. Rather, the marketing communications staff, which took direction from product or market management groups primarily, developed them. Yet, the objective of most campaigns was to generate inquiries for sales. No wonder the sales group followed up these inquiries in a hit-or-miss fashion, as salespeople weren't involved up-front in the process and therefore had no real commitment.

This traditional approach to marketing communications can no longer survive, as it lacks not only targeting but measurement as well. The following is a new approach to campaign planning based on the imperatives of the new sales coverage model. Many of the traditional elements remain, but the approach is quite different, as it relies much more heavily on targeting, segmentation, and delivering messages with offers that drive specific behavior. It is also tightly coordinated with the sales group.

Direct Marketing Leads the Planning Process

One of the major shifts in campaign planning is that for B2B marketers, target marketing or direct marketing leads the campaign process and is supported by advertising, PR, trade shows, and so forth. This is a dramatic flip of the traditional approach. Previously, marketing communications people first thought of how to create awareness of the product or service and then directed their agencies to create advertising and PR programs to accomplish that goal. So, eye-stopping graphics and cute headlines were created in the hope of leaving the reader with some type of idea regarding what the product or service was and which company was selling it. Generally, these ads focused on the product or service and contained few, if any, benefit statements. Since the message had to fit all the readers, it was concentrated on "us" and not the customers. The ultimate telltale sin was the common closing line containing the phrase "for more information" and the instruction to circle the reader response card, call this number, or visit the website.

This process was not only lazy marketing but also a colossal waste of money! Few inquiries were generated, and even when inquiries were received, the response and follow-up was slow or nonexistent. (This was discussed in Chapter 6.) Only as an afterthought did some direct marketing occur. This usually happened when the marketing communications manager was sitting with the trade magazine sales representative and, as an inducement to run a bigger schedule, the rep offered to throw in the list of subscribers. "Great," said the marketing manager, not knowing what, if anything, marketing would do with the names. When the list arrived, a direct mail communication was thrown together that looked and sounded much like the advertising. The agency also was charged with creating, printing, and mailing this direct mail piece, and since the agency people weren't direct marketers, self-mailers with no letter or offer were frequently sent. OK, I might have gotten carried away a bit with this scenario, but it's not too far from the truth, even today.

That brings us to the next question: what should be the new campaign planning and execution process to achieve greater results and properly integrate with sales? That's what this chapter is all about. It is not about creating the actual communications, as there are lots of books on direct mail creative, Web design, and telemarketing script writing. Rather, the chapter presents a step-by-step process to help you develop the direct marketing campaign and integrate it with sales.

The Four Elements for Direct Marketing Success

There are four widely accepted elements in a direct marketing campaign that bear on its success. Knowing each element and the impact or leverage it has on the campaign's success is the foundation of the planning process.

List (50 Percent to 70 Percent of Success)

The targeting and segmentation process leads to an understanding of which companies and individuals should receive the communications. The problem in B2B is finding a list that matches the target. In consumer direct marketing an interesting twist occurs. A good list (this means that it has proved to be responsive) becomes a "market." So, consumer direct marketers are in search of new lists to expand their markets. In B2B the reverse is true. We know who the market is; we're in search of a good list that describes the market. In addition, if the list is not accurate or targetable, those who receive the communication will often have no interest in the product or service. Finally, the accuracy of the list controls the delivery of the communications to the right individual within a company location. Therefore, in B2B the list is far more important than in consumer direct marketing and should consume a commensurate share of the time and attention in the planning process.

Offer (20 Percent to 30 Percent of Success)

The offer, or why someone should respond, is the second most important element in direct marketing success. A compelling reason to "act now" that is related to the product or service is critical to driving the desired behavior. The principal offer types are detailed in Chapter 6. Don't be swayed by a product manager who feels that the product being offered is the offer. The product is the "offering" and not the offer, as far as direct marketers are concerned. For technical products, this can be a difficult discussion if those responsible have fallen in love with the technology and believe that it will sell itself. We all know that's not true, so the goal is to arrive at an offer that compels the right individual to respond now.

Sequence and Frequency of Contact (15 Percent to 25 Percent of Success)

We have a great advantage over consumer direct marketers in that the value of the sale and customer in B2B is so much higher that we can afford to contact potential and current customers multiple times. Therefore, the sequence of the media of communications and the number of "hits," or frequency, becomes a key ingredient in the campaign planning process. There are only three media from which to choose that have the characteristics of being both proactive (we control the "when") and targetable (we can send the message to specific individuals, or the "who"):

- Mail
- Phone
- E-mail

I've not included fax because it is fast becoming a legacy communications medium. If it works for your business, then put it under the mail category, since when delivered, it is handled and distributed like a mail piece. With these three primary media in mind, ask yourself: should we start with a mailing followed by a phone call, or vice versa? If you have the person's E-mail address and some level of permission to use it, you have additional options on sequence. The most effective combinations now are E-mail and phone (in either order). In years past, the leading combination was mail and phone. Test out what works best in your market.

One note on sequence: the option of using phone first and then mail may seem a bit costly to most marketers. While it is true that a completed telephone call is five to ten times the cost of a mailing package, consider the benefits. If you call first, you will be able to determine if the individual on the list is still with the company and in the same job. If you learn that the contact name is no longer valid, an immediate list cleanup occurs, and the names of any replacements for the job function can most likely be ascertained as well. In addition, a brief message can be left with the individual that your company is sending an important communication and to be on the lookout for it. Then, within twenty-four hours, have the mailing sent first-class. Try this approach as a test to see if the list cleanup and subsequent response rates justify the extra cost.

The "frequency" is simply the number of times you "hit" the target with a communication. Hits aren't always different media; you can "hit" the target multiple times with the same medium. In my experience, three times in a compressed period (two to four weeks) is the most cost-effective frequency to generate the highest cumulative response rates. Going beyond three hits in a short time frame usually does not produce cost-effective response rates.

These two elements are deployed in combination to drive response from the targeted individual. Mix them up—you'll be surprised at the result.

A few comments on seasonality are also applicable here. In consumer marketing there are definite times to launch direct marketing communications and times not to. The best months for results in consumer direct marketing historically have been January and February—not November or December. The reasons offered for this seemingly illogical fact are many, but in general, the most widely accepted are that, first, consumers know both what they have spent on Christmas and what they got, so they are filling unmet needs with their available money, and second, the "hut" factor takes over in the North as winter weather causes many people to spend more time inside, and thus more attention is paid to mailings (particularly catalogs) and other direct marketing communications (for example, response TV).

Do we have seasonality in B2B? This question is usually asked as the Christmas season approaches and clients begin to shy away from initiating a campaign that would hit from Thanksgiving through New Year's Eve. Just as in the consumer segment, the facts seem illogical. Direct marketing campaigns launched during this time period, and particularly around the Christmas weeks, produce higher response rates. Hard to believe? I not only have proved this on several occasions but also can offer the following three reasons to explain this surprising result:

1. While the holidays do interfere with normal business, they also have another effect, and that is that business travel and activity slowly die down as we approach Christmas. Therefore, more of our "targets" are in the office with fewer meetings to attend and can pay more attention to direct marketing communications. In essence, B2B has its own "hut" factor.

2. For companies whose fiscal year starts in January, this is a normal time for individuals to begin to consider the upcoming year and the changes to be made and things to be done. In this mental state, people are more open to new products and services than they are during the other months. Also, a pronounced downtime occurs between Christmas and New Year's Eve as people clean up their offices, decompress, and, from our viewpoint, are more available to engage in direct marketing communication.

3. Fewer marketers are communicating, as they are also shying away from this time frame, and the communication clutter falls off dramatically. Without all this clutter to contend with, your message and offer have a high chance of breaking through and making an impact. Therefore, don't shy away from the holiday time period—use it to your advantage.

On the other hand, the end of the summer is a relatively bad time to hit businesspeople, since many are squeezing in the last summer vacation. In Europe during August most everyone is on vacation. While the situation is not that bad in the United States, there is a downturn in response rates in August.

Creative (10 Percent to 15 Percent of Success)

When I give my seminars or presentations and the subject turns to the Four Elements of Direct Marketing Success, I usually ask if there are any creative directors in the room. That's because I know that when the slide with the percentages shown here appears on the screen, I may be the target of a well-thrown rotten tomato. It is not that creative is not important to the communication; it's just that other elements in the campaign are more important! Poor creative can sink a campaign just as fast as anything, but this element needs to be pragmatically considered in the context of the other elements. The bad news is that most agencies first think of the creative execution and not the other elements. So, what happens in B2B is that too much focus is placed on the creative execution, and the other elements become afterthoughts. This will lead to poor results, and that's one reason that creative is worth only 10 to 15 percent of success.

The "creative" is usually composed of three parts: copy, art, and format. This obviously applies more specifically to direct mail than to E-mail and certainly telemarketing. Copy in B2B is king and should lead the creative development. The problem is finding a capable B2B direct marketing copywriter. If you do find any, care and feed them, as they are worth their weight in gold. The format of the mailing piece is second in importance. In fact, years ago, we had a creative director, Kevin McCann, who first folded paper before he even drafted copy or directed layouts. When I asked Kevin one day why he did this, his answer was great: "If people don't find the mailing piece interesting, they won't read it!" What he was trying to do was create interest in the way the mailing package appeared when readers first looked at it before they even read anything. More on creative later in this chapter.

The Intersection of the Buying Process and Campaign Planning

The first chapter briefly mentioned the buying process versus the sales cycle. For campaign planning, this relationship needs to be expanded a bit further. Here's the key issue. In most marketing communications, the assumption is that all people hearing or seeing the communication are at the beginning of their buying process. Thus, inquiries are treated accordingly. The reality is that, unless the product or service is truly new, not all individuals are just beginning to consider the solution being communicated. In fact, many are engaged in selecting a competitive solution at the very moment they see or hear about your product or service. Therefore, if we are to replicate the sales model more closely, consideration must be given to all the phases of the buying process in developing the campaign and communications. To review, here is a generic example of steps in a buyer's process:

Need awareness and definition
Vendor identification
Information gathering
Vendor evaluation/initial selections
Request for proposal or quote
Narrowing of vendors
Demonstration/presentation by vendor(s)
Reference checking
Vendor selection
Negotiation
First purchase
Evaluation
Second purchase

Replace these generic steps with the correct buying process for your targeted segment, and then think about not only what the message should be but also what the offers should be. I say "offers" because when the full buying process is considered in campaign planning, there usually need to be several offers to interest individuals at different stages of the buying process. The very exercise of considering the full range of steps in the potential customer's buying process will ensure that the marketing communications become more inclusive and thus effective.

Budgeting

Of all the traditional or legacy systems that need changing for the new sales coverage model, the budgeting process is the most important. Without money, our world doesn't go around! Since, historically, marketing communications did not assume a truly important role in achieving sales results for B2B companies, the budgets were not only small but also improperly developed. Here are some of the traditional budgeting methods I've encountered in the last twenty years. How many of these are all too familiar to you?

• **Last year plus or minus some percentage (usually 10 percent).** With no real analysis having been completed, the budget for this year is based on last year, with an adjustment for the company's overall results: poor results—a deduction; good results—an increase.

• **Set percentage of sales.** At some point in history, it was said or dictated that marketing could or should spend a set percentage of the forecasted sales revenue. In B2B this percentage usually varies between 1 percent and 3 percent—a low rate compared with consumer marketing budgets, which can top 30 percent. The rationale is that sales does the real work, so why spend any real money on marketing communications?

• **"Gut" budgeting.** Usually someone without any experience in marketing but who is in a position of authority just "feels" that the marketing budget should not exceed a certain amount. When pressed, this individual defends the dollar decision by stating, "That's all we can afford." Of course, the "affording" part is based on the person's gut feeling or insecurity about spending real money on marketing. This, at times, is coupled with the sad fact that if the marketing budget were significant, someone would ask for a justification or, worse yet, a measurement of what was achieved with the dollars. Since advertising and PR are historically impossible to measure, it is best to keep them at low levels so no one will ask.

• **Copycat budgeting.** The question asked is: "What are the competitors spending?" Once this is determined, it is easy to just copy their budget, adjusted for the relative size of the company. The implied hope is that the competitors are smarter, and even if they aren't, it is a plausible defense of the budget amount if asked.

Clearly, there is a need to establish budgets that bear some correlation to achieving results. The good news is that with the direct marketing process now leading the way, there are several new approaches that are far more logical. Here are the three basic inputs to establishing more soundly based budgets:

1. **Breakeven analysis.** To understand just what is at stake and how much can be spent on a marketing campaign, the first number to establish is breakeven. Simply, it is a calculation of the amount of sales revenue (at gross margin) that must be achieved to pay for the

campaign. First, establish the revenue of an average sale that is at stake. For example, here's a recent client situation in which the average sale was worth $100,000 and the gross or contribution margin was 40 percent, or $40,000. Based on this margin, how many sales would it take to pay for the entire cost of the campaign? The campaign was calculated to cost $47,000 including all agency fees. Therefore, the number of sales required to fully liquidate the campaign cost would be slightly more than one. The question then to answer is: Is one reasonable to achieve? Well, the target comprised 504 hospitals in California, and it was very reasonable to assume that at least one sale would result. Remember that the sales required to reach breakeven is not a goal or objective of the campaign. It's just an evaluation of the reasonableness of the budget.

2. **Allowable cost of acquisition.** This common direct marketing calculation is a judgment regarding how many dollars we can afford to acquire the customer. On the cost side, it calculates the cost of not only the campaign but also the lead-qualification effort and the follow-up effort by the sales group. On the revenue side, the calculation also values the customer beyond the initial sale and, while not full lifetime value, usually adds up the yearly potential. The resulting budget then is shared by both marketing and sales, and measurements are taken against this "allowable" cost. In the preceding example, the client had additional revenue for services and a cross-sell opportunity. As a result, the total yearly customer revenue added up to $175,000. At 40 percent gross margin, the margin was $70,000, and the director of sales and marketing felt that the company would support $10,000 to acquire this customer revenue and margin. Now we're talking some real dollars for an integrated campaign.

3. **Expense to revenue, or E/R.** The reason for this measurement is that few companies really calculate return on investment. They talk about ROI a lot, but if you ask an accountant to calculate it, the formula becomes too complex for marketing purposes. So, the E/R calculation is a placeholder for ROI. It's simply the number of dollars spent on the entire campaign as a ration to the number of dollars in revenue generated. Normal ratios in B2B are between 1/10 and 1/20. Over 1/20, you're doing extremely well. In the ongoing example, we expected a 10 percent qualified-lead rate, meaning the percentage of

leads that result directly in a sales presentation. Our experience with hospitals was that for every three sales presentations, one close would occur. Here are the numbers:

504 hospitals × 10 percent lead rate = 50 sale presentations
50 presentations × 33 percent conversion = 16 sales
16 sales × $100,000 in revenue = $1,600,000 and $640,000 in margin
Campaign expense of $47,000/$1,600,000 revenue = 1/34 E/R

Sure looks like a winner to me! That aside, the point of presenting all these budget approaches is to arm you with practical tools so that the budgeting process will be based more on what's at stake versus the old and badly outdated systems of establishing the budget.

The Campaign and Creative Briefs

Because direct marketing campaigns are more detailed and integrate the lead process and sales group, there is a need for a sound campaign plan. Most of the template that follows is logical and refers to prior material and information that you may already be using. This outline of a campaign brief is presented on the basis that one or two sections may provide some additional insight for you to apply when developing a campaign plan that fits your marketing situation.

Campaign Plan (Outline)

- **Campaign goals and objectives:** What larger goal or program does the campaign support and what specific objectives will be measured?
- **Targeting and list selection:** What companies and individuals are targeted? Give a description of the lists that have been researched and selected that match the targets. This should include any house lists as well.
- **Offer strategy and specific offers:** What offer strategies (soft, lead development, or hard) and specific offer(s) have been developed for this campaign?

- **Contact strategy:** The sequence and frequency contact strategy and timing of each.
- **Creative:** See the Creative Brief that follows.
- **Testing plan and rationale:** What elements are to be tested and why? How will this learning be used in the future?
- **Response handling and offer fulfillment:** Who will handle the responses and what is the expected turnaround time to fulfill? In addition, what is the offer to be fulfilled and how will this be accomplished?
- **Lead criteria and qualification process:** What BANT levels are set to qualify a lead and how will this be accomplished?
- **Sales handoff procedure:** How will the salespeople or distributors receive the leads and what is the system and requirements for feedback?
- **Flow control:** How will the leads flow to sales and/or distribution and what is the expectation as to the number per week or month?
- **Flow chart:** A flow chart of the campaign.
- **Budget:** The overall campaign budget.
- **Measurements of activities and results:** What measures of success will be tracked for both activities (response rates) and results (sales) and the time frame of the measurement?

In my experience a campaign plan, when written, creates a great deal of discussion among all the groups involved. These discussions and resolution of issues and questions are the most important aspect of the plan. Discussion catalyzes coordination and cooperation and will set the stage for a much smoother campaign.

While the campaign plan is key to success, the creative brief referenced within this plan is also critical to success. This assumes that an outside agency or creative resource will be retained to develop the direct marketing program. Here's the issue: most creative people are not familiar with most of the products or services sold to other businesses. This is particularly true if the product or service is technical or complex. Therefore, the input they receive is all the more important for their understanding and subsequent creative development. I've seen numerous executions totally miss the mark when the creative team didn't understand the nature of the industry and product or service solution. The creative brief bridges this gap.

Creative Brief

The sections that need to be filled out are listed here along with explanations of what to include in each. There is some duplication with the campaign brief, since these are separate documents for different audiences.

- **Target audience description:** Describe, in some detail, the target audience by position or function. If there are several decision makers and influencers, list each one.
- **Key fact:** Provide a short statement or distillation of the current marketing situation or environment and the most important fact or issue confronting the marketing group.
- **What marketing problem must the direct marketing campaign solve?** Be candid, and speak from the company's perspective. Try to identify the core concern(s) or reasons not to buy from the viewpoint of the target audience.
- **What is the objective of the campaign?** The objective, in part, flows from the marketing problem. The objective should be quantified, with a time frame attached to the result. Also state what type of response rates are required to reach the objective.
- **What is the most important benefit or promise offered by the client that the targeted audience must believe?** This benefit must be strong enough to address the marketing problem and also meet the objective.
- **What facts support this benefit or promise?** Why should the businessperson believe the proposition? This needs to be a straightforward listing of reasons and facts. Supporting documents should be attached or referenced.
- **What negatives may the targeted audience cite about the benefit, promise, or use of the product or service?** What barriers to a decision may exist in the minds of the buyer? Is there any reason they may feel that this type of product or service doesn't solve their problem? Remember that a great degree of skepticism now exists in most people.

- **Who is our competition?** Include both direct and indirect competition. Indirect competition can also be defined as the budget and the lack of desire to change, or status-quo attitude.
- **What are the advantages and disadvantages of the product or service?** These should be referenced against the competition as listed in the previous question.
- **What action do we want the target audience to take?** Desired actions usually include calling, mailing, website visit, trade show visit, and so forth.
- **What stage of the buying process are we targeting?** The typical buying process has several steps. These should also be detailed here so that the entire buying process is known.
- **What offers do we feel will incite the target audience to take action?** In essence, what will move the audience from the targeted stage of the buying process to the next?
- **What tone and manner should the direct marketing have?** Use specific adjectives to describe the desired look and voice of the communications. Should the communications match the approach of any other established creative or past efforts?
- **What items are mandatory?** What must be included, such as logos, 800 numbers, or specific colors?
- **How will the success of the campaign be measured?** While response rates are important benchmarks along the path to a sale, they are not sufficient measurements of success. What is the campaign trying to achieve in terms of sales? How long will the campaign be given until a final measurement is required on results?

Testing

Testing in B2B is rare. Why? For one reason, the number of targets in any campaign is frequently too small to generate enough responses to assure statistically reliable testing results. Also, testing usually requires treating one person or company differently from another. This can cause concern among sales and product management, as they don't want to deal with two different types of responses or offers. Having said that it is rare, testing is still a smart course. Then the next question quickly arises: what should we test? Before you can answer that question, there are several perspectives to consider.

First, the major elements of a direct marketing program are the best areas for testing. In quick review they are:

• **List.** One of the easier and most common tests to execute, as no changes in the other elements are needed to perform a list test. All that is required is to match responses back to the original lists.

• **Offer.** The offer is an important element to test because it can dramatically change the results of a direct marketing campaign. A little bit later in this chapter, I'll detail an offer test we did for J. I. Case Farm Equipment that demonstrates the importance of the offer and its impact on response rates.

• **Sequence and frequency.** This is another test that typically does not require changes in the creative package and can also have quite an impact on the results.

• **Creative.** Creative is probably the last element to test, as it not only is costly to change but also has the lowest impact on results compared with the preceding three elements.

The second perspective to consider is what may be called "wide variation" testing. By that I mean that if you're going to test, make the variation on what is tested great. It's not productive, for instance, to test two different white papers; instead, test a white paper against a Web seminar. Big differences in the test will create readable differences in the results.

Third, the testing method can incorporate one of several approaches. Here are three possibilities:

• Use A/B split testing, in which an equal number of randomly selected targets are treated differently. Usually the split is 50/50, but other percentages can be used if needed so long as the cell size is large enough.

• Send the communications to a small sample of the target audience, and then measure and assess results to see if they met expectations. If expectations are not met, another small test can be constructed and repeated. This can be done either in a random fashion or by taking a representative geography first, followed by other geographic locations. Given that B2B campaigns frequently involve sales follow-up, the geographic testing approach can work, since only one or two territories need be involved. In fact, the territory to consider for the test may well depend on who is covering the territory and whether or not he or she will participate in the test and provide feedback.

- If all of the foregoing procedures seem too difficult and slow, then a focus group can be used to "test" the offer and even the creative. Remember that focus groups are not quantitative, so be careful in extrapolating the results. Years ago, I held a focus group for a company selling an office product to office managers to test the offer that would be the most appealing. To everyone's surprise, the offer that the client (a male who had never been an office manager) felt was best was the least favorite of the three offers among female office managers. Actually, the real reason for conducting the focus group was that I felt we didn't really know what would be appealing and the client was so sure he was right. Well, you should have seen his reaction when his idea was soundly panned.

Finally, while this is not a course in statistics, I offer a simple rule of thumb to keep in mind. Try to obtain at least thirty—and better yet, fifty—responses per test cell before believing that the result is valid and repeatable. So often, the testing quantity is too small to generate the number of responses required for any statistical validity. Remember that the reason for the test is to determine which variation works best, so you don't want any false reads from the test that then can't be repeated.

A "Case" Story

A number of years ago, we were given the assignment by J. I. Case to develop a database of the top 100,000 farmers in the United States. Public data gathered from the government provided the number of acres and type of crop grown, but none of the information we had contained the type and age of equipment on the farm. Case sold farm machinery, so it was essential to have this information. As an example, when a tractor reaches seven years in age, it is about ready for "retirement." Even the company's database on warranties had only partial information, since sales were made through distributors. Therefore, a survey sent to the farmers was the only way to gather the data we needed. We sat around and discussed what offer(s) would motivate farmers to list all their equipment along with make, model, and year—for large farms, this was a lot of equipment. Using the philosophy of wide variation testing, we finally settled on the following five offers to test. All included the same survey for completion.

1. Upon return of the survey, respondents would receive a free booklet or audiotape entitled "How to Pass Down the Family Farm"—a key issue for farmers—written by an estate planner who specialized in family farms.
2. The survey mailing package contained a pen flashlight with a Case logo and a note that said, in effect, "Thanks in advance for filling out the survey, and keep the flashlight."
3. Upon return of the survey, the respondent would receive a coupon for a free family portrait at Sears—no strings attached.
4. The survey mailing package contained a dollar and a note of thanks with the suggestion, "Buy yourself a cup of coffee while filling out the survey." (This was before Starbucks.)
5. Upon return of the survey, the company would make a $10 donation to the respondent's local chapter of Future Farmers of America, in the farmer's name.

In Racine, Wisconsin, where Case is located, there were about ten of us sitting in the office of Steve Kopp, the marketing communications manager, when we made the final selection of the offers to be tested. Steve pulled out a dollar bill and asked all of us to do the same. Then he passed around Post-it notes and asked each of us to write our guess as to which offer would win and stick the note to our dollar. The stack of dollars was then sealed in an envelope by his assistant and filed away. Eight weeks later, the results were all in. Here's the winning offer and the percentage breakdown of the responses:

1. **Dollar bill.** 56 percent response rate
2. **Pen flashlight.** 36 percent response rate
3. **Sears portrait.** 18 percent response rate
4. **FFA donation.** 16 percent response rate
5. **Estate planning tape.** 12 percent response rate

With some anticipation, Steve opened the envelope to find that only one person of the ten had guessed the winning offer. Most people had guessed the estate planning tape and the FFA donation—the two worst-responding offers. The moral of this test is twofold:

- If we had taken a vote and selected the offer that the majority thought would win, the results would have been almost 45 percent less than achieved—a big miss, by any standards.
- The only way to find out what works is to ask the customer, not the client or agency. We are all too close to the situation, and besides, we are not the buyer.

A footnote from this "Case" result is that guilt works. For both of the top two test offers, the offer was included in the mailing package and, if kept, gave the farmers a sense of guilt if they did not return the survey. By the way, we got back surveys with the dollar enclosed—farmers are truly the "salt of the earth"!

Flowcharting

One of the most helpful actions that can be performed in campaign planning is creating a flowchart of the process. As the details of a campaign are many, a flowchart helps people to visualize the process so that they can follow it better. Figure 9.1 is an example of a flowchart, using the hospital campaign cited earlier.

Flow Control

I've borrowed the term *flow control* from my chemical engineering classes, since in B2B it can be important to "flow" out the leads to the salespeople. That's because, on average, without any unusual pressure, the salespeople will give you approximately 10 percent of their time for lead follow-up. This also means 10 percent of their calls. Therefore, if a salesperson makes 3 calls a day (the current average) and is in the field 46 weeks for a total of 184 selling days (holidays, vacations, and meetings are deducted from 52), this calculates to 552 sales calls a year. If 10 percent can be devoted to leads, then 55 calls per year are available, or only 4.5 per month—roughly 1 per week.

So, if a large lead-generation campaign is developed and executed without an eye toward flow control, then the potential to overwhelm the

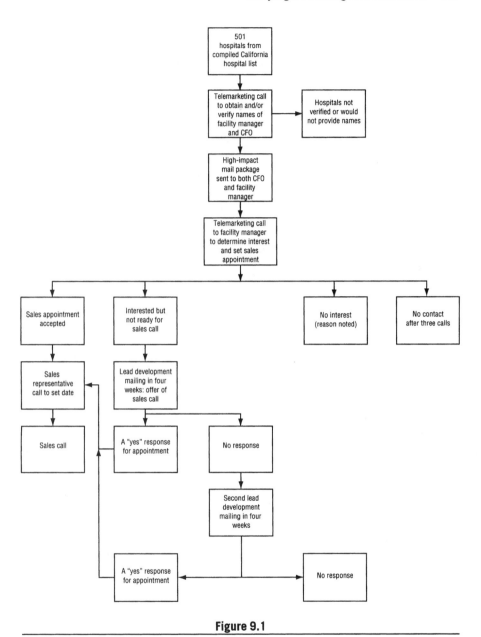

Figure 9.1

sales force or distributor exists. Many might feel that this is a problem they would be glad to deal with (particularly if prior lead programs have not produced high response rates). In fact, this might be just the problem that sinks the campaign if a salesperson is sent five, ten, or more leads per week to follow up on. The salesperson will most likely call on only one, since salespeople have other important calls and duties to perform. Is it any wonder that leads don't get followed up, even if the salesperson feels they are good leads (which most salespeople don't)?

This all leads (no pun intended) to flow control. Reverse-calculate the number of leads that can be followed up by sales back to the number of inquiries that need to be generated and all the way back to the number of mail pieces or telephone calls. Here's an example based on what are average and realistic response and conversion rates:

200 mailing pieces $\times$ 5 percent response rate $=$ 10 inquiries
10 inquiries $\times$ 10 percent qualification rate $=$ 1 lead

Now plan your campaign drop and execution around the flow control.

This approach represents one of the biggest opportunities for improving campaign results, as very few programs that I've seen take into account these factors. What usually happens is that the campaign is started with great impact to generate the most responses as quickly as possible. Hopefully, a lead-qualification step is included (frequently it is not), and the leads are sent to sales. We calculate the response and lead rates and congratulate ourselves on a job well done. Only later does someone ask if we know the number of sales or revenues attached to the campaign. We contact the salespeople who got the leads and inquire. They generally report that the leads weren't any good. Why? Because they didn't even follow them up and are not going to tell us that. I can't really blame them too much, as nobody took into account their job responsibilities and time pressures. We just dumped leads on them and said "go!" Not really the way B2B campaigns should be integrated with sales.

Thinking about flow control will go a long way to resolving one of the problems. In addition, another interesting thing happens if the salespeople get only one or two leads versus more than a handful: they value each one a bit more if they have only one or two. The analogy I make is that leads should be more like rare eagles than common pigeons.

Setting Up the Back End

In general, we do a much better job at developing the campaign and launching it than at setting up the back-end and fulfillment processes. Yet, a Performark study several years ago (referenced in Chapter 6) documented that the single most important element to improving sales conversion was speed of response and fulfillment of the offer. How long does it take to respond to someone who has found our message and offer compelling and actually said yes? Here are some scary thoughts:

- If someone responds to a magazine ad or direct mailing, studies have shown that seventy-two hours later the individual has forgotten that he or she responded.
- A recent study on response time from Web inquiries showed that it was worse than mail responses—and they are poor.
- More than 20 percent of all companies that ask for responses in their ads or direct marketing efforts don't respond at all!

The Performark study referenced showed that if the response time was accelerated to twenty-four hours, the rate of conversion to sale rose by an eye-popping seven to ten times. What wouldn't we pay for that kind of lift to any campaign? Yet, most B2B campaigns are launched with little thought or effort directed to what has to be done once the inquiry is received.

Several years ago, I was asked by Digital (soon thereafter to be Compaq and now HP) to help figure out what was wrong with a campaign, as the salespeople were in revolt. I went there with the anticipation that this would be a great new and profitable client. Was I wrong. After only a few hours spent learning what they were doing, I found the major problem. Here was the inquiry-handling process:

1. All inquiries were sent to the advertising manager and recorded and counted.
2. These inquiries were then sent to the product group for review.
3. The product group then sent them to the regional sales manager for distribution to individual salespeople.
4. The regional sales manager then passed them to the salespeople for follow-up.

The salespeople were reporting that when they called (now almost two months after the individual responded), the person either denied responding (having forgotten) or had already bought a competitive computer. While this story is several years old, it is still being played out today. Recently I talked to managers who had leads from six months ago and were wondering if they could still give them to the sales group—you can guess my answer!

Speed of follow-up is critical, and I recommend that twenty-four to forty-eight hours be your standard turnaround time, no matter how the inquiry arrives (mail, phone, or Web). One response technique to consider is to call or E-mail responders and tell them that the inquiry has been received and that a response is on its way. By doing this, you potentially open up the opportunity to ask a few more questions (be sure not to overdo it) and, more important, ensure that when your fulfillment package arrives, the individual pays closer attention to it.

The reason that a fast response converts to higher sales is twofold. First, you capture the interest of the individual and therefore can begin the sales process promptly. This helps assure you of the highest possible lead-qualification rate, and certainly you will beat the competition to the punch. Second, it reflects positively on the company, as the potential buyer will infer that your company "has its act together." Confidence in the company from which we may buy is a key determinant in the sale.

Finally, lest we forget, responses have to be recorded on the database or some other record-keeping system, which needs to be set up prior to the campaign kickoff. Frequently a list test is also part of the campaign, and it is imperative that the capture and recording of the responses be accurate in order to find the best-responding list. Responses may arrive in a variety of media, and all response points (mail, phone, Web) must be included. Unfortunately, most of the systems in the tele-center and Web generally are not linked into the database, so the "recording" may be, in part, manual. So be it, as this is a vital back-end step.

Postmortem Campaign Analysis

The final step in effective campaign planning and execution is, believe it or not, an analysis of what happened. This is so obvious that it almost begs not to be included in the book. However, less that 20 percent of the time do I see a formal analysis undertaken for the purposes of learning and modification of next efforts. We are all so busy that, once the campaign is done, the campaign results are all we know.

Plan to gather all involved parties in a postmortem session. This is not a finger-pointing session but rather one in which all concerned are looking to analyze everything for improvement. In fact, the "best practices" usually come from these sessions. Another benefit is that all of the individuals involved in the analysis will bring different points of view (for example, the telemarketing manager versus the campaign manager), and the very interaction will promote closer working relationships in the future. It is a team-building exercise as much as it is an analysis of the campaign.

Summary

Campaign planning and execution takes time, and frequently we don't give it the due it deserves. In the past, marketing communications didn't need to link as closely to sales as they do today, and so they just planned for themselves. This close linkage now places a much greater premium on careful planning so that all the moving pieces and parts work together.

The major benefit of the planning process is the engagement of the sales group, product management, and distributors in the plan. This engagement process will be more beneficial to the marketing group than any other element, since when they are asked for input prior to the campaign being executed, they feel committed and will become more willing partners. The most common complaint I hear from clients is that the sales group didn't provide the requested and needed feedback. And why should they? It wasn't their idea. We all laugh about the phrase "not invented here" and, in this case, it has meaning. Involve the sales and product management group in the campaign plan and creative brief and you will have a much tighter team that believes in the campaign and will be invested in the results.

Campaign planning and execution in the B2B world is much more complex than in consumer. It must be done thoroughly to have any chance at success. All the moving pieces of the campaign must be carefully coordinated, since the failure of any one can spell doom for measurable results.

10

How to Build
Your Company's Database

FOR BUSINESS MARKETERS who have attempted to develop a company's database, the experience has typically started with high expectations and enthusiasm that then degenerate to frustration and partial results. It's not a pretty picture for those of us who evangelize the strategy of database marketing. Even though these initial efforts are rocky, the need to create a functional database has never been more important to achieving tough marketing and sales objectives and efficiencies. The emphasis on customer relationship management (CRM), targeted marketing, and measuring results is increasing, and a fully functional marketing database will be necessary as the supporting tool.

First, a perspective on this strategy should be mentioned. The phrase "database marketing" is two words, and both are active ingredients in successful marketing programs. Too frequently, emphasis is placed either on the "database," with the result that few marketing executions are done; or on "marketing," with the result that the database is nothing more than a poor list. To truly achieve the results initially projected when this approach is undertaken, you need to align the database and marketing pieces so that one of these elements does not outpace the other.

175

So, the march toward real database marketing continues, and this chapter will help those who have already started this process and provide initial guidance for those who are just beginning to build the company's marketing database.

Where Are Most Companies Today?

Based on my experience, here are some of the issues facing most everyone:

• The attempt to pull together the current internal data has been all but impossible due to different software systems and formats (for example, accounting files and lead lists) as well as inaccuracy and incompleteness of the data.

• Members of the sales group resist providing the needed data because they don't have some or all of it on an electronic format (it's in their heads and on paper) and/or don't see the benefit to themselves in spending time complying with marketing requests for customer and prospect information.

• The team that was assembled to define what was needed for the database had too many people and functional groups, and it overreached in defining what data elements should be included. The result is that it could take months, if not years, to gather all the data that were deemed important.

• The accuracy of the internal data turned out to be extremely poor, as updating information has never occurred. There is no consistency in the manner of recording data, and many of the records are incomplete.

• The attempts to enhance the internal files with outside business information such as SIC code and company size proved to be difficult and produced low match rates.

• The software that was purchased or written for the database project doesn't have all the functionality that is needed, and additional software or expensive customization is now required.

• The database-building project is taking longer to complete, is way over budget, and will not reach the ROI goals that were set to justify the initial budget. Worse yet, people don't feel comfortable using the database or can't properly respond to requests for certain data or programs.

Now that I've got your head moving up and down, you're probably thinking about another job within the company, or even a complete career change—and if you're just starting out to build a database, you're probably looking for the nearest exit. Well, it's not going to be easy, but what follows are some pragmatic suggestions, procedures, and sources of solutions that just may save the day (if not your job!).

Establishing What Data Should Be in the Database

When creating a marketing database is first discussed, there are certain logical data elements that everyone agrees should be included. These are customer information and the sales history. Beyond that, the other data elements and the rationale for adding them become a little less clear and many times rely only on the opinions of the people working on the project. Therefore, often too little or too much data are included, and this becomes clear only when the database evolves into usage.

What is needed at the outset is a data strategy that serves as a method to distinguish between what is truly necessary and what is desirable to have on the database. In addition to customer information, the key issue for usage is the ability to target and segment current and potential customers so that relevant communications can be delivered to these prospects and customers. Therefore, what follows is a guide for determining what data to include on the database.

Customer Information

The specific information contained on the customer record will be somewhat different for each database, but some elements should be consistent. Here are some choices and decisions to make:

• **Address.** This category may seem too logical to mention, but for larger customers there may, in fact, be several addresses (for example, shipping, accounts payable, and the front door). Public information will have the "front door" address as standard. Accounting may have a problem with this choice if the billing address (frequently a P.O. box) is different. This means that careful consideration of the address field of the company is required. For most databases a designation of the type of site (headquarters, plant, research laboratory, et cetera) is also important. In addition, a linkage should be established for multiple sites or divisions of the same company. Dun & Bradstreet's D-U-N-S numbering system is a great help here.

• **Contacts.** Attached to each company location are the important personnel contacts for the buying process. In fact, many databases are organized so that the contact name is the primary record and is rolled up to site location and/or company. Keep in mind that titles, while important, can be misleading and frequently do not define people's responsibility at their companies in relation to buying your product or service. Thus, the database should record the title for communication purposes but also list the function performed that is defined by the sales or buying process you employ to obtain customers. Sometimes decision maker versus influencer is a designation worth including, in addition to function. There can be much discussion on other information regarding contacts, such as one of the sales staff's favorite—birthday. This kind of information belongs on the salesperson's records and should not be on the marketing database unless it has a projected use in future communications.

• **Industry.** For decades the industry definition has been the Standard Industrial Classification, or SIC, code. In 2000 this officially changed to the North American Industrial Classification System, affectionately abbreviated as NAICS. There are several improvements contained in this change and two that are significant. The first is the addition of specific new classifications for high-tech companies, and the second is the consistency of codes in Canada and Mexico. You should contact a business list compiler such as D&B, InfoUSA, Experian, or the Department of Commerce to learn more and determine how best to include the new system in your marketing database.

• **Company size.** Another essential demographic fact is the size of the customer or prospect. Many times, the dollar revenue is desired, but this figure can be inaccurate and hard to obtain. Of the 10 million or so companies in the United States, only 10,000 are public. A better and more easily obtained definition of company size is the number of employees who work at the site and/or company. Both the dollar volume and employee count are, at times, modeled by the business list compilers but are generally accurate enough for database marketing. The reason for using employee size is that this piece of information is easily obtainable by asking people within the company, while the actual revenue figure may be closely guarded or known by only a few people. Therefore, you will be able to determine size of customers and prospects more easily by just asking for employee counts.

• **Transaction or sales history.** The two issues that need to be defined in this important area are what level of detail on the sale of the product or service is required to be on the database, and how far back in time the record should go. If your company has warehoused the complete sales history of its customers, then this decision is a bit easier. A way to help set this level of depth is to ask what the usage will be in future marketing and sales programs. In general, the amount of sales history that is actually used is less than originally thought, so be conservative when deciding how much to add to the database. Consider summarizing this information and/or deleting details that are not appropriate for database marketing. The good news is that this type of data does not change or decay over time if the original input is accurate.

Other Standard Demographic Data

• **Economic indicators.** At times, the area of the country or state has an economic health or growth factor that may be important to target campaigns. This could be extended in the database to a growth indicator of various SIC or NAICS codes. Both the Department of Commerce and Federal Reserve publish this type of economic information.

• **Credit rating.** This piece of information is provided by firms that track companies' credit and payment history and can be of importance if you have a product or service that experiences problems with bad or slow payments. Service businesses are particularly alert to this situation, as once a service is given, the "value" is reduced, and slower payment may result, which, of course, strains cash flow.

• **Company age.** The number of years in business may help indicate company stability or even creditworthiness. It may be particularly important if you have determined that life cycle segmentation is a predictor of the opportunity for a sale. Newer companies also exhibit different behavior from mature companies.

• **Fiscal year.** If the sale of your product or service has to be budgeted by the potential customer, then knowing what fiscal year is in place may be of paramount importance, as the budgeting cycle will be dependent on the fiscal year. About 80 percent of public companies are on a calendar fiscal basis. The other 20 percent are spread between the first, second, and third quarters. If the business is not a C corporation, then the fiscal year must start on January 1 to align with personal tax periods. This is true of Sub S corporations.

Relational Demographic Data

Relational demographic data are factual information that is relevant and specific to the sales of your product or service. As a way to explain this very important data choice, pretend that you are selling plastic raw materials. In this case, the kind of processing equipment (extrusion, blow molding, et cetera) would definitely be important to include on the customer or prospect record. If, on the other, hand you are selling commercial bank loans, a typical relational demographic would be whether or not the prospect has filed a Uniform Commercial Code (UCC), which indicates the pledge of assets for collateral on a loan.

One way to ascertain what data elements would be excellent relational demographic fields is to involve the sales staff in the process of developing your database. Ask salespeople what they would like to know about a company before they walk through the doorway. It's this key sales information that would alter their sales approach that you want to capture on the marketing database.

One of the reasons that this information can be of chief importance is that your competitors can also obtain the SIC or NAICS code and employee size from public databases, but chances are that they won't have this type of relational demographic information. This gives you the communication opportunity to not only segment the audience differently but also create messages and offers that are much more relevant. We know from test after test that the more relevant the message, the higher the response rate.

Outbound Communication Flags

The database should contain enough open fields to record when the targeted individual has been sent a direct mailer, an E-mail message, or a telemarketing call. Additional fields should be included to properly record the nature of the message and offer. This will not only equip you to segment based on what the target audience has been sent in prior communications but also serve as the basis for analysis when a response or sale is the result of a series of communications.

Stage of the Sale or Buy

Of course, if the field force is using a sales force automation (SFA) package, salespeople are recording the call dates and other information that is important to their direct sales efforts. Here is where some cooperation between marketing and sales can really pay off. Not only should the people who are called on be listed, but also a definition of each person's function and role in the decision process should be recorded to facilitate future marketing communications.

Further, the firm that is called on could fit into possibly one or two categories in either your selling process or their buying process. The first, and more common, is the stage of the selling process. Here's an example of this definition:

- Inquiry
- Qualified lead
- Proposal sent
- Sample sent
- Final negotiations
- First sale
- Multiple sales
- Long-term customer
- Past customer

The second category is the stage of the buying process. The difference is that most companies have a predetermined selling cycle that usually *does not relate* to the customer's buying process. This becomes even more apparent when any segmentation is applied to the marketing database. Here's a standard example of how the buyer may describe its process:

- Need awareness
- Information gathering
- Setting specifications/request for proposal
- Requesting quotations
- Supplier qualification and interviews
- Trial/sample run
- Supplier selection
- Price/contract negotiations
- Contract signing
- First purchase
- Initial performance evaluation
- Repeat purchases
- Valued long-term vendor

The outline of this buying process may be nothing like your situation, but going back to the plastic raw material example, the selling process and the buying process could truly represent the same sale. Notice that there are more steps in the buying process than the sales cycle. (I've found this to be true in almost all cases.) Also, the terminology is quite different. The point is that all buyers will feel more comfortable when the seller mirrors their process and does not try to sell them in a manner that is "out of step" with how they are going to purchase. Marketing and sales communications based on the buying process are far more relevant and powerful than those grounded on the company's sales cycle.

Response Behavior

Among the most crucial database fields is the one that records the appropriate information on responses received from direct marketing or other sales and marketing efforts. Outbound communication is great, but what's even better is having the targeted individual respond. Not only mail, phone, and E-mail responses should be captured but also attendance at trade shows, seminars, and conference calls. All the "touches" accumulate to a behavior, and it will become increasingly important to record the touches and tie them to the customer's behavior in a manner that provides insight into what programs and combinations work most efficiently and effectively.

In addition, customers and prospects remember what they have done and, frankly, think your company should remember their actions as well.

They really don't expect it, however, as few companies have the ability to record and reference prior behavior when talking to customers. Just think of the reaction and delight the individual would have if you cited his or her prior interactions with you in your next marketing communication. Not only would it amaze the customer or prospect, but it would also change the nature of your communication, offer, or other subject. At this point, your database is beginning to drive that fabled but almost never achieved one-to-one relationship marketing.

There are many other data options and potentials, and as you proceed down this road, they can be added. Right now, though, look back at the preceding data elements and visualize the multiple campaigns and messages that could be launched from what you've got. I think you would agree that this would make your direct marketing programs extremely targeted and productive. In the end, it's the smart use of the data in database marketing that produces results. This array of data will enable great results!

Sources of Data

Once the initial selection of the data elements has been determined, the underlying subject of just where the data will come from needs to be fully explored. In fact, if certain data cannot be sourced or would be too expensive to obtain, you may not want to include those elements on the database. In business marketing we face a more daunting challenge than those in consumer marketing, as the data obtainable on companies and individuals within those companies is far less accurate than consumer information, and it changes or decays faster. This situation is compounded by the fact that the U.S. Post Office does not track individuals who change companies but, of course, does follow us as we move our personal residence, via the National Change of Address (NCOA) system. So, the following sections describe the three primary data sources to consider in the pursuit of the most accurate and complete data for the marketing database.

Internal Sources

It is ironic that, at times, the most difficult sources to obtain are, in fact, internal lists and data that currently exist. Before the advent of database marketing and enterprisewide CRM systems, these internal sources resided in different locations and/or software and were there for different reasons. Here's a rundown on the typical situation before the dawn of database marketing and CRM.

Accounting or Customer Files Most companies think they have an accurate customer file, as the recording of the sales and billing system *must be* the customer file. While that is true in some respects, what is often found is that the address is for billing purposes only, and the name on the record is the person responsible for paying the invoice. This may be an accurate customer record when the customer is very small, but as the company size increases, the accounting record becomes less representative of the sales or buying process.

Much important information, though, is contained on this file, such as the sales history. The issue is that it may not be the correct address for marketing and sales contacts. The file is even less likely to include the names of key decision makers and influencers. On the other hand, you can't alter this record to eliminate the needed billing information. Therefore, selective download from this accounting system is required for input into the marketing database.

In the late 1990s, I experienced an extreme example of battling the accounting department in one of the country's largest software providers. This firm, which will remain nameless for obvious reasons, recorded on their master customer record the name of the individual who signed the contract. As these contracts were for multiple years, the names on the master record were there for multiple years as well. When we went to mail the customer record, only then did we discover that many of these individuals were no longer there or in different departments. On two occasions, the individuals had died; we found out upon receiving a letter from the company saying, "He's no longer with us"—literally. Yet, the accounting department strongly resisted changing the master customer record, as these were the "official" signing names on the contracts. Needless to say, we didn't use the master customer record.

Marketing Lists or "Databases" Over time, the marketing department accumulates various lists that are derived from advertising responses, trade shows, and even direct mail efforts. While the lists may be recorded on the same software (for example, Access or Excel), they have never been merged and de-duped and are treated as separate lists. In addition, purchased or rented lists may also be available internally if they were purchased for unlimited usage.

The important perspective here is to realize that these are lists and not databases and need to be merged with customer and other information to form the overall marketing database.

Sales Staff Contact Information Today most sales groups have gone to some form of SFA software (such as ACT), and the information that is recorded can be worth gold. Unfortunately, the salespeople generally don't employ strict data-entry rules, which can cause much variation from salesperson to salesperson in what is contained. In addition, not all fields will contain data, as different salespeople may or may not feel that a particular field is important to their sales efforts. Also, much data will be in the "comments" field and therefore inaccessible. A final problem is that the field software is usually not structured enough to be used as the marketing database. All these issues need to be dealt with before this key information is uploaded into the database.

Customer Service Contacts/Records Much like the sales staff's usage of SFA, most customer service departments have their own software and data-entry approaches. This information can be as valuable as sales records, since it frequently uncovers a variety of issues that can be used in customer retention and up-sell efforts.

Obviously, these four internal sources, along with any others you may have, need to be merged into one view of the prospect and customer. It is not the purpose of this book to offer methods and recommendations on software and procedures to do this, but I can offer some advice: do not try to do it internally no matter how good the MIS group claims to be. Business data merging is tough stuff and requires special software algorithms and much experience. Find a capable outside resource to partner with, as this will save you much time and money. See the Resource Directory for firms that will perform this function.

Keep in mind that the faster you can use the database and achieve results, the more support and budget the database marketing program will receive.

Public or Outside Information Providers

Fortunately, in the past several years, business data compilers and owners of response lists have seen the potential in business marketing, and we now have a better and more accurate selection of information. There are several types of business information suppliers:

Business Information Compilers A business information compiler gathers data on the entire market by drawing from a variety of sources. The most common source is the business white and yellow pages. Credit files and notices of incorporation are additional sources of information and may be used in conjunction with other methods of gathering demographic data.

The key advantage that compilers have in the business market is that the lists have most, if not all, of the companies in the United States and even other countries. This total market coverage can be critical when your marketing database needs to describe all the potential companies in a given segment (by geography, SIC code, company size, et cetera). Also, typically included are the names of the senior executives for each company. This is generally good enough for companies with fewer than ten employees, but of course, as the size of the company increases, the "president" may not be the appropriate person for your direct marketing program to target.

There are only a few companies that thoroughly compile business information:

- Dun & Bradstreet
- Experian
- InfoUSA

Each has good data and some differences and uniqueness based on the company's method of compilation and updating. It's best to talk to all of them and match your needs with the proper business information compiler.

Response Lists By definition a response list is a recording of people who "do something" or respond. This response could be as minor as sending in the qualification card for a free trade magazine, attending a trade show, or, in more classic direct marketing fashion, buying a product or service. There are thousands of response lists, and a good list broker or a subscription to the SRDS Mailing List Directory will provide you access to most of these lists.

The key advantage of these lists is that they have the name, title, and address information of the individual who has responded. Typically such people are not found on the compilers' lists unless they are the company president, the company owner, or a senior executive at the specific business location. The weakness is that usually no other company information, such as SIC code or employee size, exists on these response records.

Co-Op or Merged Lists Several cooperative lists and databases have recently emerged. This trend is a result of the desire of marketers to have both the demographic information of the compilers' lists and the name depth of the response lists.

The best example of this type of emerging co-op list is MeritDirect in White Plains, New York. Merit has a list of over 42 million names of individuals attached to more than 16 million companies gathered from hundreds of participating B2B catalog firms. The best news is that they have enhanced this response list with SIC, sales revenue, and employee size information from two major business compilers. The result is the best of both worlds, a combination of response names and demographic information. To make this even more usable for B2B marketers, they have developed analytic tools for profiling and segmentation. MeritDirect is, therefore, one of the best sources of B2B data and services in the marketplace. They are referenced in the Resource Directory in both the "Top B2B List Sources" section and the "Computer Service Bureaus" section.

A few years ago an article in *DM News* reported that Grainger has brought together several companies that are selling to the same industry but do not compete with each other. They are sharing their customer information by using an outside computer service bureau to hold the merged list. This helps to safeguard the integrity and confidentiality of each company contributing its customer records. There may be opportunities for you to engage in much the same program. The recommended approach is to enhance the merged co-op list by using one of the business compilers' databases as the platform to overlay all the sales contact information of the companies participating in the co-op database.

Another way to tap outside or public information sources is to identify the several lists that target your market and then have them brought together or merged by a computer service bureau experienced in business marketing databases. As mentioned before, this process is not something that should be attempted internally. In most cases, the lists that you select will be a combination of compiled and response lists.

Primary Data Gathering

It's no surprise that the best source of business information on your targeted list of prospects and customers is the companies themselves. In essence, much of your customer and prospect records and lists have been derived directly from some form of contact with the respective company. The problem is that the records have not been gathered with a database or direct marketing in mind. Therefore, what you need to do is to reverse the process and begin to identify and obtain data primarily for the database. Your internal sources, such as the sales staff and customer service, should be alerted to the required data and asked to alter their process to help obtain the missing information.

Another approach not to overlook is to enlist the aid of the specific individual and/or company in obtaining the information through surveys or some form of direct request. The Internet can even play a new role here. One opportunity is to send an E-mail to individuals who have a relationship with your firm that shows what information you have on them and then ask for updates and corrections. Remember that you should have some form of relationship and should express your rationale for asking for their assistance. People have a hard time not correcting information on themselves that is inaccurate.

A new method to update names has recently become available. The method is interactive voice mail and the company with the best solution is SoundBite of Waltham, Massachusetts. One of the applications of their new technology is calling the individual on your list and using a message recorded by someone in your company to request an update on information. Additional information can also be communicated and, therefore, this low-cost interactive approach could be valuable on several marketing fronts. There are other applications of their technology. If this sounds (no pun intended) interesting, they are referenced in the Resource Directory in the "Telemarketing Services" section.

There may be other methods that you can develop. The point is to not rely only on outside data providers but to enlist the aid of the prospect and customer as well.

Updating the Database

Unfortunately, once all the jobs are done and the database is ready to run like a race car, it quickly begins to misfire and requires continual tuning, much like an old Jaguar. The issues are twofold:

1. What data must be updated and how often?
2. What is the method for updating each important element?

The best method for answering the first question is to establish the "decay" rate of each of the data elements and combine it with the importance of the element to establish a priority that will allow you to arrive at the optimal frequency of updating. As an example, based on research that our firm has conducted continually over the last eight years, 70.4 percent of businesspeople undergo one or more changes in their situation (business card) in a twelve-month period. It splits almost down the middle, with 31 percent changing companies and the other 39 percent changing jobs or locations within the same company. If accuracy of the contact name is critical to your sales, then this data element needs updating on an ongoing basis. Other data elements, like SIC code, do not change. So long as they are initially correct, the only updating would be the recording to the new NAICS system, as previously discussed. This is an area in which a business list compiler could also be of value.

As to the updating methods, they are as many as you can think of! There is no magic bullet, and all the methods you can employ at reasonable cost should be used. Here are some that you may not have thought about:

• Once a year, send your customer data file to the best contact on the database and ask for corrections and additions. This could be hard copy or E-mail or both. You may want to include some form of "thank-you" at the time of the request.

• Also try this approach for the mail room of larger companies, since it's these employees who have to handle mail that is addressed incorrectly or to people who no longer work at the company. Call and ask for the name of the mail room supervisor, and send this person a small token of appreciation along with your listing of their company and the request for updates.

- When you participate in trade shows, take along a PC and a copy of the prospect and customer database. When someone stops by and is willing, have the person review the record for his or her company and make corrections.

- Ask the customer service department to inquire about certain data elements after successfully providing the service.

- Run your list through the National Change of Address (NCOA) system, as companies move just like people.

One warning: Do not send a list of customers and prospects to the sales group and ask for the list to be updated! This will not work and, in fact, is not their job. Of course, there is nothing wrong in picking up changes that are recorded as the natural result of their sales effort. Help the salespeople, and do not burden them with "another stupid request" from the marketing department.

The Value of the Data

Finally, I have a few words about the importance, or value, of your data. In my experience, companies have little problem spending large sums of money on software and even hardware to house the database. In many cases, however, they are reluctant or even unwilling to spend much money on the data. Somehow they expect that in the normal course of business the data will not only flow in but be kept accurate as well. This never happens, and many times, the company's data are so bad that the post office can't even deliver the mail. Recently I worked with a company that sent out a catalog (at $2.50 each) to its customers and hot prospect list. To everyone's surprise, 35 percent of them were returned! Obviously, the postage cost was high, but the lost sales opportunities were incalculable.

To paraphrase a recent political line, "It's the data, stupid." An old direct marketing axiom is that a great program and offer sent to a bad list will not do as well as a bad program and offer sent to a great list. Try this and you'll find it to be true. Another thing to remember is that most experts agree that 60 to 70 percent or more of the results of a business direct marketing effort are due to the segmentation process and list selection that matches that segment. A smaller percentage of success is due to the offer, creative, and media.

If a sales call now costs, on average, $350, how much would a lost sales opportunity cost? Obviously, a powerful leverage to creating sales revenue is the completeness and accuracy of the database. So, educate everyone on the value of the data and the need to spend money for obtaining the best information and keeping it updated. If you are successful, not only will your job be easier, but the smart use of the data will drive the company's revenues to new heights.

Summary

"Database marketing" is two words, and this chapter has been all about the first word—the data. In B2B, one of the most difficult challenges is to achieve data accuracy and completeness on not only the customers, but on prospects as well. Over the last twenty years, we have evolved from finding lists to developing our own databases, but the primary issue remains the same—we need a good list! The single most important element to success in direct marketing is the list. Most industry experts put its importance at 60 to 70 percent of success. Therefore, if you are going to spend money on marketing communications, you should spend money on the data. I frequently consult with clients who do not have any data hygiene processes in place to update their customer list, let alone the prospect list. This is shortsighted at best. On the cost side, money will be saved by not sending communications to people or even companies who should not be targeted, or who may not even exist. On the revenue side, think of the lost sales opportunities when individuals and companies who should receive your communications do not! Put them together and you have some real improvements that can be achieved by spending the appropriate time and money on the data and the database.

11

How to Measure the Results That Will Sell Management

IN THE PRECEDING chapters much has been outlined as to what to do. The other shoe in our environment now is "What happened?" Management is no longer tolerant of being able to measure one result—sales. So, when it comes time to justify the marketing communications budget, the major result that produces identifiable revenue is the leads that have been generated and turned over to the sales groups for conversion.

That's when the problems start. First, what to measure is called into question. On one end of the spectrum is the recorded data that marketing communications has on the number of raw inquiries and qualified leads handed to the sales group. On the other end are the sales groups, whose members will point to only a few leads that were "worth anything." That is, of course, if they will even admit that there was a lead that they didn't already know about. The upshot is that no one can agree on what result to measure.

Second, how to measure the flow of an inquiry all the way to a sale is fraught with even more problems. When inquiries and/or leads are sent to the sales group, they frequently disappear into a "black hole." At best, some feedback is obtained from the field, but almost never is the feedback system tight enough to track all the inquiries or leads to their final disposition. Therefore, no closed-loop process exists, and thus, no measurement of any result is possible.

This chapter details the best practices found in B2B marketing and sales today. Obviously, the identification of "what to measure" and "how to measure" requires customization to any company's situation and "go-to-market" business model. What follows is a solid foundation to not only start the internal discussion but provide a measurement "ladder" to climb as well.

In addition, any system that is constructed needs to be fully discussed and agreed to by all members of marketing and sales, since without consensus it has virtually no chance of actually working. Many good attempts have failed for this very reason. The marketing communications department cannot propose any process that the sales groups don't think is in their own self-interest. Otherwise, the sales group's skeptical view will surely doom any potential measurement system, because the salespeople will never close the feedback loop.

Finally, in today's environment in which most business initiatives focus on productivity, the lead process has more opportunity for dramatic improvement than any other area in the entire B2B marketing and sales arena. When this process is fully tested and delivering information, companies will achieve the seemingly impossible twin goals of "selling more" by "spending less." The knowledge gained as to which programs and campaigns produce the best results will introduce the marketing communications department to a new world of marketing insight.

What and How to Measure:
The Measurement Ladder

You may be surprised at the relatively large number of measurements from which to choose in the inquiry-to-sale process. Starting at the ground level and proceeding higher, these measurements could be called a "measurement ladder." The goal is to reach the highest possible rung. Here's the complete measurement ladder sequentially organized by *activity*, *value*, and *result* measurements.

Activity Measurement
- Cost per thousand, or CPM

- Response rate
- Cost per inquiry
- Cost per lead

Value Measurement
- Value per lead
- Value of market opportunity from the campaign

Result Measurement
- Breakeven
- Number of sales
- Dollar value of sales
- Expense to revenue ratio, or E/R
- Return on expense, or ROE
- Lifetime value, or LTV

Activity Measurements

This category of measurements is frequently the only one that is calculated, as the data reside in the marketing communications department and therefore are more easily accessed for calculations. The problem is that activity measures only give quantification to a marketing activity and cost of that activity. Therefore, they do not satisfy the management question of "What are we getting for our money?" Many years ago, when asked, John Wanamaker uttered his famous observation, "Half the money I spend on advertising is wasted, and the trouble is I don't know which half."

Activity measures lay the base for the more important calculations of *value* and *results*.

Cost per Thousand The CPM is one of the most common advertising and marketing measurements, as it simply states the cost to communicate to or reach one thousand people. When you're purchasing magazine advertising, this CPM number allows the comparison of the cost to reach one thousand readers among different magazines. When used in advertising, this number can be misleading, as it is unknown just how many of these one thousand people actually see or read the advertisement, but it is nonetheless a useful planning and analysis advertising statistic.

In direct marketing the CPM is much higher than in advertising. For instance, if a letter package costs $0.75 each to mail, then the CPM is

$750, versus a typical advertising CPM of well below $100. This number in direct mail usually does not reflect the cost of the agency but rather just the monies needed to produce and mail the package, or variable cost. At times, the agency and creative costs are included if the mailing is not to be repeated. If the package is to be remailed, these one-time charges could be amortized over the total number of mailings to arrive at a CPM that reflects both the fixed agency and variable costs.

Either way, the CPM is an expression of the cost to, hopefully, reach one thousand individuals in the targeted audience. Much more can be written about this number, but what can be distressing is when someone in the marketing communications department feels that reducing the cost per thousand is a good objective. It is not! In fact, frequently the higher the CPM, the more effective the campaign. The CPM number should be known but otherwise not used in measuring marketing communication results.

Response Rate   This common measure is almost exclusively used in direct marketing, as it is the first measurement demonstrating a result of a targeted communication. The advertising world does not want to use this calculation, as response rates would be so small as to undermine the value of advertising to effectively generate inquiries. Of course, creating awareness or brand building is generally the rationale for advertising in most cases. Simply, response rate equals the number of responses divided by the total number marketed to by mail, E-mail, or telephone.

A simple example:

$$\frac{250 \text{ responses}}{5,000 \text{ mailed}} = 5 \text{ percent response rate}$$

This number, while useful, can be misleading, as no evaluation of the quality or sales potential contained in these responses is possible. In direct marketing the offer for responding is the key determinant in the quality and quantity of responses. Offer strategies are another important subject, but the debate in developing offers is this balance to be struck between quantity and quality of responses desired. If the offer is of low risk and high personal value to the targeted individual, then the response rate will be higher. A free sleeve of three Titleist golf balls will generate lots of responses, but the quality of the responses will likely be low if the target is engineers for CAD/CAM! On the other hand, if the offer is for a sales presentation within one week, then the quantity of responses will be very low but the quality extremely high.

All marketers do attempt to increase response rates, and there is nothing wrong in this objective, as many times, the larger number of "fish caught in the net" will improve final results. This is particularly true if the product or service is new, as a wide net should be cast when you're introducing new products.

Cost per Inquiry This measure is the first in the line of cost measurements that, if calculated, can also alert managers to the high cost of lead generation (more about that later). Again, the costs in direct marketing are usually only those associated with the variable costs of producing and launching the mail, E-mail, or telemarketing program. The costs are then divided by the raw number of inquiries or responses to arrive at the cost per inquiry. In the preceding example, a 5 percent response rate was achieved with a mailing package that had been relatively high in impact and, thus, cost. Therefore, let's assume a cost of $2.75 per package. This cost is then multiplied by the five thousand pieces sent, for a total of $13,750. The cost per inquiry is as follows:

$$\frac{\$13,750}{250} = \$55 \text{ per inquiry}$$

A good use of this measure is in comparing different marketing communication efforts. This comparison could even be extended to trade shows, seminars, or advertising. It is not a measure of quality but rather a relative measure of the cost to generate inquiries. If the target audience and the offer remain constant, then it is a good measure to judge the effectiveness of each of the media or campaigns launched against the audience.

Cost per Lead Now, here is where some of the fun begins. It starts when the question of "What is a qualified lead?" is asked. Here's a good exercise to try. Ask three or four individuals in the marketing and sales organization what they would define as a qualified lead. At least three or four different answers will most likely be received. So, the first job is to define a qualified lead in terms that can be agreed to be all. This is not a lesson on how to determine the definition of a qualified lead but rather an aid in obtaining agreement. Here are the four most common criteria used in developing the definition of a qualified lead:

- **Need** level for the product or service
- **Timing** of the purchase decision
- **Authority** of the individual to make or influence the purchase
- **Budget** available to purchase

Each of these four areas is also subject to various definitions, as each product or service offered will have different qualification definitions and parameters.

Once the qualification criteria have been established, the next task is to contact and qualify all those inquiries to see if they meet these preset criteria. This sounds simple but in practice is rather difficult. Most often an outbound telemarketing effort is started to talk to the individuals who responded. An E-mail effort can be combined with this telemarketing effort if the E-mail address has been given by the responder with the understanding that it may be used for further communications—in other words, permission marketing. Frequently the combination effort will produce the highest contact rate.

So, let's take our example one step further. But first, this "cost of lead" calculation needs to consider several other issues:

- Any follow-up effort also has a cost, and that should be added to the cost side of the equation. Let's assume a telemarketing follow-up at $40 per hour and a call completion rate of two per hour. Remember that callbacks will be needed, and that's why only two completions per hour are estimated. Therefore, every inquiry contacted now costs another $20.

- Even with three callbacks, not every inquiry will be reached. After three attempts, a reasonable percentage reached may be 70 percent. We will use that for our calculations. So, of the 250 inquiries, only 175 will be reached and qualified based on the preset qualification criteria.

- Not all inquiries will be at the same stage of the buying process or progress through the sales cycle at the same rate. Here is where many lead programs are suboptimized, as some inquiries are not yet at the point of being able to meet the definition of a qualified lead. That doesn't mean that, given some more information and/or time, this inquiry will not become a qualified lead. This is called *lead development* and is covered in Chapter 6. For calculation purposes, this extended process is not factored into this example.

Keeping these issues in mind, normally 10 to 20 percent of all inquiries will become qualified leads. Remember that this is without a lead development effort in which more of the inquiries may become qualified. Studies have shown that approximately 30 to 50 percent of all B2B inquiries will buy the product or service they inquired about within twelve to eighteen months. There's more "gold" in those inquiries!

Let's assume that 20 percent of the inquiries contacted are found to be qualified, as we'll assume this campaign had excellent targeting and a great offer. Using our prior statistics, the cost per lead would be calculated as follows:

250 inquiries $\times$ 70 percent contact rate = 175 completed calls
175 $\times$ \$20 for telemarketing = \$3,500 additional cost
20 percent qualification rate $\times$ 175 inquiries = 35 leads
\$13,750 campaign cost + \$3,500 telemarketing cost = \$17,250
$$\frac{\$17,250}{35} = \$492.85 \text{ cost per lead}$$

This may seem like a high cost, and maybe it is, but all too often companies have not calculated true lead costs. Frankly, it is not unusual to have a lead cost exceed \$1,000 each. The knowledge of the real lead cost will alert the sales groups as to just how much money has gone into each lead before they received it. It is hoped that this will add motivation to their follow-up and feedback efforts.

Value Measurement

A new calculation has recently begun to close the gap between the number and cost of leads and sales revenue for measuring marketing communication results. The problem is that, while it is desirable to measure actual sales and return on expense or investment, the sales cycle frequently is far too long to suit management's desire to know if the campaign worked. Thus, many lead measurements are attempted before all the leads have had a chance to convert to sales. As a consequence, many lead programs are measured only against partial sales results.

In addition, the prior measurements of inquiry and lead costs do not indicate the potential sales and profit margin contained. When faced with "costs," all managers want to reduce the figure. Thus, what frequently happens is that year after year, the objective is to reduce the cost of the inquiry or lead without any reference to the "value" being created. Therefore, those forward-thinking companies that want to support and grow lead campaigns and sales are attempting to put a value on the lead, versus just a cost.

Value per Lead This approach requires a reference to a prior campaign with known results. Another approach is to calculate a lead-to-sale model that places a value on the lead. Here are the questions to answer in building a value-per-lead measurement:

• How many qualified leads can be reasonably expected to convert to a sale? National averages for lead conversion range from 10 percent to 30 percent. The conversion percentage will depend on the strictness of the lead-qualification criteria that are used to define the qualified lead.

• What is the average sales volume for this type of customer? Sales volume has three levels to consider. First is the initial sale. Second is the yearly volume that assumes repeat sales. Third is the lifetime value of the customer. All of these will be discussed later.

Keeping with our example, let's say that 20 percent of the leads qualified should convert to a sale and that the average sale is $50,000. Only the initial sale will be used for calculations in this example even though many firms use the annual volume. Several firms use lifetime value. Here's how this calculation is developed:

35 leads convert at 20 percent, for 7 sales
7 sales × $50,000 = $350,000 revenue
$$\frac{\$350,000}{35 \text{ leads}} = \$10,000 \text{ value of each lead}$$

Since we didn't know before the conversion-to-sale effort which of the thirty-five leads would turn into the seven sales, we place the "value" on all leads that have been qualified. This allows for a value measurement much sooner, which therefore can be used to answer management's question of "What did we get for our money?"

Value of Market Opportunity from the Campaign   Once the value per lead has been established, a logical extension is to add up all the leads and project a value of the total market opportunity created by the campaign. One approach is to use the $350,000 as the "opportunity" created.

However, this figure references only the seven sales that are expected to be closed by the sales group. In reality, all the leads developed represent the total market opportunity. The competition will sell a portion of these qualified leads, since the buyers will most certainly be checking out alternate sources and solutions as well. In addition, not all leads will actually buy, as budgets are cut, projects are put on hold, or the needs disappear for some other reason. Therefore, another calculation is possible, and in our example it would be as follows:

35 leads × $50,000 per sale = $1,750,000

Remember that this initial campaign plus the lead-qualification cost totals $17,250. Compared with either the $350,000 in the expected seven sales or the $1,750,000 in total market opportunity developed, this expense certainly looks small.

The point in the calculation of these two value measurements is that the discussion between marketing communications and management is now dramatically altered. What's occurred is that instead of talking about "costs" and the need to reduce them, the discussion is now about "value" and how to produce more! This is a meaningful change for all marketing communications people to achieve, as it now places the emphasis on the production of results and not the costs to get there.

These new "value" measurements will be difficult to develop, since they require some forecasting of results and represent a new concept in B2B marketing communications. The potential here is great, and even the opening of the discussion to develop value measurements will highlight the *results* of a lead program and not the costs—a much-needed change in the dialogue!

Result Measurement

Results, in terms of sales revenue and margins, are what lead programs should be all about. The primary interface between marketing communications and sales has been the lead system, but over the years, it's been mostly a one-way street. Marketing handed leads or inquiries to both sales and distributor groups and then went back to get more. The sales groups looked at them, called on the ones they felt were important or interesting, and tossed the rest into the "to do" folder—if not the "round file." Unless extreme pressure was exerted on the sales group, the feedback to marketing was either partial or nonexistent. Therefore, no real measure of final results was possible. Frequently stories of individual lead results (both good and bad) circulated and were used as anecdotal evidence far too often as a measure of just how well the lead program was performing. What follows are several result measurements that require a feedback system from the sales groups.

Breakeven   Breakeven is a traditional direct marketing measurement that is frequently not calculated in B2B. Simply, it determines how much has to be sold to pay for the campaign—in other words, to break even. It is not an objective to achieve but rather a benchmark. In consumer direct marketing, knowing the breakeven is a fundamental piece of knowledge, as it is always used to throttle the campaign spending. In B2B the breakeven percentage is usually unknown.

The calculation is simple but has one decision that can be difficult: what "margin" should be used for the sale? The debate is between the gross and net margin. The gross margin is usually determined by subtracting just the variable cost of manufacturing from the sales revenue. It does not include overhead costs and therefore is higher than net margin. The net margin is what is left after all variable and fixed costs are subtracted from revenue. Obviously, it's lower than gross margin. Traditional consumer direct marketers use gross margin to calculate breakeven, as they contend that the revenue created by the campaign is incremental and therefore does not carry the overhead costs with the activity.

Let's look at our example to see how both calculations may appear:

$50,000 sales revenue
At 50 percent gross margin = $25,000 margin
At 15 percent net margin = $7,500 margin

What's the breakeven using the $17,250 lead-campaign cost and both margin figures?

$$\frac{\$17,250}{\$25,000} = 0.69 \text{ sales required to reach breakeven at gross margin}$$

$$\frac{\$17,250}{\$7,500} = 2.3 \text{ sales required to reach breakeven at net margin}$$

Obviously, by using the gross margin, you need fewer sales to "pay for" the campaign expense. The problem is that this approach is a tough internal sale to management and particularly the CFO. What is required, though, is an agreement on the "margin" percentage that should be used for the breakeven calculation. The good news is that in almost all B2B situations the number of sales required to pay for the campaign is very low. This realization will give the marketing communications group more ammunition to use for budget justification and garnering sales management support.

Finally, the breakeven is usually expressed as a percentage. Using the 2.3 sales required divided by the 5,000 mailed would yield a 0.046 percent conversion rate to reach breakeven. In any marketing circle this is a very low success rate and one that should be easily achieved.

Breakeven can be a powerful piece of information and is very helpful in assessing if the marketing communications budget is too high or (as in most cases) too low. Here's a story that exemplifies the point. The client is a large chip manufacturer for whom, over the years, I had consulted on developing their database and lead systems. I was also creating an internal training program for them, so my visits were somewhat frequent. Just prior to one trip, I got a call from one of their marketing communication managers and was asked to spend a few hours assessing a direct mail project that they had executed but from which they'd gotten almost no responses. It was a big problem, as the new manager of this group had predicted a 10 percent response rate.

When I entered the room, they tossed me the mailer and said, "Why did it fail?" "Hold on," I said, buying some time to think. "Before we jump into the mailing piece can I ask a few questions?" "Sure," they said.

Here's what I asked: Who are the targets? How much is an average sale? What is the margin of the sale? How much did you spend on the campaign?

Here are the answers. The target was current customers. They were introducing a chip upgrade to these customers, and they had slightly more than five thousand of them. The average sale, over a three year life cycle, would be approximately $100,000. As this was an upgrade, gross margins were high at 75 percent. They spent $35,000 on the campaign.

I was stunned and didn't hold back. "You mean that one sale nets you $75,000 in gross margin? Then how many sales did you have to make to pay for the entire campaign?" The room went silent, and the manager who had forecasted the 10 percent response rate looked up a bit sheepishly and said, "One-half," adding, "I guess you think we didn't spend enough?"

"Well, yes," I said. "If it were me I would have sent each of the five thousand a dozen roses or something like that." I then asked why the budget was so small in comparison to the pot of gold at the other end and the answer was all too familiar—"That's what we had to spend." And yet, if they had calculated the breakeven I'm convinced that this calculation could have been used to justify a higher budget from management.

Now, there were other problems with the mailing piece: the fact that it was a self-mailer with no letter, that the offer was buried in mice type, and so forth. But the *real* problem was that they didn't fund the effort properly, and were therefore reduced to having to do a self-mailer. They budgeted themselves into a corner.

This is a problem I see all too regularly. By calculating the breakeven, you can first assess whether or not the budget makes sense, and return to the "bank" for more if it doesn't—but now, you'll have some convincing ammunition.

On the other hand, occasionally I do see campaigns that are over-funded and there is not a chance in purgatory to break even. On these campaigns, a reassessment of the plan is needed as well. Frankly, in B2B I seldom see this scenario. It almost always is too little money.

Number and Dollar Value of Sales These measurements now seem self-evident, since in the preceding examples we needed to estimate the number of sales converted and the dollar average per sale. However, remember that those were estimates. Now we're talking about the actual number of sales and dollar revenue.

Arriving at these numbers requires a feedback system to obtain information from the sales or accounting groups. As pointed out, the actual number and dollar volume of the sales may take a long time to determine. This is a critical subject, and discussion and agreement with sales management must take place before these measurements can be implemented and used to judge campaign success. Put simply, just how long should the lead be considered a lead? In other words, how long is the average sales cycle for the specific product or service?

All too often the desire to quickly measure overrides the knowledge that some leads have not converted. Thus, the success of the company's lead-generation campaign will be understated. In addition, there is usually a gap between the company's view of the desired speed of the sales cycle and the buying process of the customer.

The central issue for developing effective result-measurement systems is that some reasonable time frame needs to be established before the sales measurements are considered final. This can be complicated by the accounting periods by which most firms live. There is always a need to justify the annual marketing communications budget when the yearly planning cycle comes around. The irony is that the potential customer and the customer's need to purchase have no relationship to the internal biorhythm of the annual planning cycle. As a result, many result measurements are taken prematurely. The only answer to this difficult quandary is to establish the average sales cycle and apply it to the "age" of the campaign to estimate final results. In this way a more realistic measure of success is demonstrated, versus shortchanging the campaign due to premature measurement. Completing all of this is no easy task and may require considerable internal discussion and compromise. Nonetheless, there is a strong reason to measure all the sales that have occurred from leads generated.

One final issue needs to be considered by all marketing communicators. Be very careful not to take sole credit for the sale, as without the sales group, the lead most likely would not have converted. Many direct marketers have fallen into the "we created that sale" trap by not sharing the result with the sales group. This is also one of the reasons that salespeople don't care to report results, as they feel that it was only their effort that produced the sale and give no credit to marketing communications—turnabout is fair play! In the end, the "lead to sale" process is an area in which each group needs to share credit with the other.

Expense to Revenue, or E/R   The E/R calculation can be a replacement measurement for ROI, as most companies talk about return on investment but never really calculate it. First of all, most executives don't view marketing communications as an investment, but rather as an expense. Second, a true calculation of ROI must consider the lifetime value of the customer, and this is also very seldom known or considered. (More about that appears later.)

The E/R measure also is easy to figure. Let's return to our example and assume that the seven sales did close. Then the E/R would be as follows:

$$\frac{\$17,250 \text{ expense}}{\$350,000 \text{ revenue for a } 1/20 \text{ E/R}}$$

This is a good E/R ratio for any B2B marketing campaign. In B2B these ratios normally vary between 1/10 and 1/25. The acceptable E/R for any company, of course, depends on a number of variables such as margin. The acceptable E/R range is another area for discussion and agreement. The E/R ratio then can be used to compare different marketing communication efforts as a real measure of cost efficiency.

Before you develop the E/R range, one other issue should be considered, and it's a big one: just how should the cost of the selling effort required to close the sale be calculated? Average cost-per-call numbers are in the range of $300 to $500 or even higher. Then, how many sales calls were required to close these seven sales? Even more broadly, how many calls were expended on all the leads passed to sales? As can be quickly seen, this question and the attached sales cost is a "sticky wicket" and is almost always avoided when measuring E/R for campaign effectiveness.

Return on Expense, or ROE   One may expect to see the famous ROI listed here, but as just mentioned, this calculation is almost never done, so the more realistic approach is to use return on expense. Here the profit or margin on the sale is the number to determine. In our breakeven example, two margin figures were proposed, and for ROE calculation the net margin is the only choice.

Using the seven sales at $50,000 each and a margin of 15 percent, or $7,500 per sale, would yield $52,500 in overall margin. Thus, the calculation of ROE is as follows:

$$\frac{\$52,500 \text{ net margin}}{\$17,250 \text{ expense}} = 304 \text{ percent ROE}$$

Not a bad return, by any standard!

Lifetime Value, or LTV The final result measurement and the one that requires the longest reach of faith is lifetime value. Again, in consumer direct marketing the calculation of lifetime value is a common and useful measure. In B2B it is rare, as it involves much added complexity and debate as to how this type of customer value can or should be measured.

Here are some of the issues causing the difficulty:

• Precisely how long should an average customer lifetime be? In many B2B situations customers have been customers for decades. Should we actually use a lifetime of ten years or so? On the other hand, some customers buy only once—how do we tell which way they will go?

• When you're calculating lifetime value, the ongoing cost of sales and service should become part of the cost side of the equation. How can that be measured without an extremely detailed cost and activity tracking system?

• If we try to use lifetime value and the lifetime is ten years, who in management will want to invest for a ten-year result when the emphasis now is on this year and next? Long-term investments are reserved for plants and equipment and not marketing communications.

There are other issues as well, but the inescapable fact is that if management recognizes that the creation of a customer has more value than just the initial or yearly sales revenue, the support for lead campaigns will increase.

A quick example may be useful here. Before the new stadium and the recent winning seasons, the Cleveland Indians were struggling with justifying the expense of their season-ticket campaign, as the results in tickets sold were minimal. Of course, the effort was launched each year in the dead of winter, when almost no one in Cleveland was thinking of baseball. By the way, most season tickets are sold to businesses, so this was a B2B campaign. To generate budget support from the owner, they turned to the calculation of lifetime value of selling a company an average of four seats. Upon their shifting the focus to the lifetime value from the yearly transactional income, the case was made, since the average length of the sale went from one year to eight years. In addition, the other income produced by the attendance—from parking, food, and souvenirs—was factored into the lifetime value. The net result was that the campaign effort was increased the next year rather than decreased.

If you want to find lifetime value, a practical suggestion is to limit the time frame used to three or four years, as most managers will buy off on this shorter period. By checking the average length of customer retention by segment, you can calculate the proper lifetime. If it's longer than three or four years, then cap it so that agreement can be reached on lifetime value.

Developing Feedback Systems that Work

Without question, the development of timely and complete feedback from the sales groups is one of the most difficult challenges faced by marketing communications people today. Many attempts have been made and failed. These efforts usually revolved around incentive programs or scare tactics by sales managers. Neither of these approaches will work for the long term.

The only system that will stand the test of time is one that creates benefit to the sales groups for their feedback. We do things that are in our own self-interest and therefore must develop benefits for sales to provide feedback. Sales group feedback is a much larger marketing and sales issue, as it extends to the accuracy of the customer database. Here are considerations and suggestions that apply to developing feedback systems:

• Most salespeople have been given "leads" by marketing that, quite frankly, weren't worth the paper on which they were written. This is a strong statement but true. This experience may even have occurred at other companies where the salespeople worked. The reason for the occurrence is that many of these "leads" were nothing but unqualified inquiries that had no sales potential. So, salespeople view more of these "leads" as worthless and do not call on them. They won't tell anyone that the follow-up calls haven't been made, so their only out is not to provide any feedback. This is not their problem. It must be addressed by developing a qualified lead program that truly passes good leads to sales. Much selling of the new and improved system is required before they will accept the leads in a different light. This represents a big effort.

- In the past, no real costs were placed on the leads, and therefore, no economic value was attached to each "piece of paper." The measurement system can go a long way toward placing such a value, but remember that an explanation of how the calculation was developed will promote salespeople's understanding and acceptance.

- Work with salespeople to develop the measurements and the feedback system, in order to obtain their commitment. All too frequently salespeople are left out of discussions at the home office until the new "system" is thrust upon them as something else to do. These "to do's" will not be done by salespeople if they are making their numbers and are secure in their jobs.

- Find as many benefits to the sales groups as possible. Benefits center on more time, more money, and less hassle.

- Finally, the Internet opens up a much easier method for feedback. Use it to the level that the sales group accepts. Don't create new, difficult, and overly complex feedback systems. The more time a salesperson perceives is required, the less likely he or she is to use it!

Closing the feedback loop is mandatory for measurement systems—good luck!

Summary

So, there it is—the measurement ladder to climb. How high to go is your decision, but obviously, the higher, the better!

Activity measurements are good baselines and are useful for marketing communications comparisons but will never satisfy the management question of what we are getting for the money spent. This question is more serious than ever before, as the focus on marketing and sales productivity is intense today.

If tracking and feedback of leads after they're turned over to the sales groups is just too difficult to achieve, then moving to the *value measurements* will bridge the gap. This will begin to effectively answer management's questions on marketing communications effectiveness and shift the dialogue from cost to value.

Finally, there is no substitute for knowing *results*, or just how many leads turned into closed sales and the revenue achieved. There are two levels of credit here. Credit first goes to marketing communications for creating the inquiry and qualifying the lead. The rest of the credit goes to the sales group for effectively selling the customer. These are two entirely different skills, and the final result is an integrated effort between marketing and sales. Neither group can or should take credit for the total result, in which each has a role. This sharing of credit will make measuring results much easier.

Resource Directory

This Resource Directory is compiled from a number of industry sources. It references firms that offer the described services and software. Of particular assistance in developing the software section was David Raab, a good friend and very smart guy who can be reached at raab associates.com. No endorsement is implied and the selection of any of these vendors and sources should be performed with the normal due diligence.

Analytics: Targeting

Analytici
150 East 42nd Street
New York, NY 10017
(212) 907-7417
Analytics and database development

DigiMine
10500 Northeast Eighth Street, 13th Floor
Bellevue, WA 98004
(425) 460-5000

digimine.com
Hosted data warehouse and data mining for customer loyalty and
   retention

MarketMiner
1575 State Farm Boulevard
Charlottesville, VA 22911-8611
(434) 977-0686
marketminer.com
Marketing analysis services and automated tools

Megaputer Intelligence
120 West Seventh Street, Suite 310
Bloomington, IN 47404
(812) 330-0110
megaputer.com
Tools for data mining, text mining, and E-commerce personalization

Salford Systems
8880 Rio San Diego Drive, Suite 1045
San Diego, CA 92108
(619) 543-8880
salfordsystems.com
Data mining and web mining tools

SAS Institute
100 SAS Campus Drive
Cary, NC 27513-2414
(919) 677-8000
sas.com
Business-intelligence software and services

SPSS
233 South Wacker Drive, 11th Floor
Chicago, IL 60606-6307
(312) 651-3000
spss.com
Turn data into insight through predictive analytics

Inquiry and Lead Generation

AdTrack Corporation
6060 Huntington Court Northeast
Cedar Rapids, IA 52402
(319) 395-9777
adtrack.com
Integrated sales and marketing support services

APC Direct
11088 Millpark Drive
Maryland Heights, MO 63043
(314) 423-8544
apcdirect.com
Inquiry and lead generation; direct-mail solutions

Business Development Solutions
139 Gaither Drive, Suite H
Mount Laurel, NJ 08054
(856) 787-1500
bdsdatabase.com
Prospecting, lead generation, market surveys, CRM services

Call Solutions
2000 Market Street, Suite 1408
Philadelphia, PA 19103
(877) 810-7171
callsolutions.com
Market research, inbound/outbound call center, customer relationship
  management

Direct Impact
12331 Riata Trace Parkway, Suite A110
Austin, TX 78727
(512) 231-8550
dirimpact.com
Inquiry and lead generation

Judson Enterprises, d/b/a K-Designers
11261 Sunrise Park Drive
Rancho Cordova, CA 95742
(916) 631-9300
k-designers.com
Inquiry and lead generation

Performark
10701 Hampshire Avenue South
Minneapolis, MN 55438
(952) 946-7300
performark.com
Web-based customer relationship management

QuantumMail.com
8702 Cross Park Drive
P.O. Box 140825
Austin, TX 78754
(800) 637-7373
quantummail.com
Inquiry and lead generation

Sales and Service: CRM

Applix
289 Turnpike Road
Westborough, MA 01581
(508) 870-0300
applix.com
Business performance management, analytics, and customer
relationship management solutions

Firstwave Technologies
Overlook III, Suite 1000
2859 Paces Ferry Road
Atlanta, GA 30339
(770) 431-1200

firstwave.com
Hosted, Web-based CRM solution

FrontRange/Goldmine
1125 Kelly Johnson Boulevard
Colorado Springs, CO 80920
(800) 776-7889
frontrange.com
CRM/SFA software

J. D. Edwards
One Technology Way
Denver, CO 80237
(303) 334-4000
jdedwards.com
Customer life cycle management solutions

Onyx Software Corporation
3180 139th Avenue Southeast, Suite 500
Bellevue, WA 98005-4091
(888) ASK-ONYX
onyx.com
CRM solutions to align sales, marketing, service strategies, and
    processes around customers

Optima Technologies
1110 Northchase Parkway, Suite 250
Marietta, GA 30067
(770) 951-1161
optima-tech.com
Customer relationship management suites

Oracle
500 Oracle Parkway
Redwood City, CA 94065
(650) 506-7000
oracle.com
CRM sales, marketing, and service solutions

Peoplesoft/Vantive
4460 Hacienda Drive
Pleasanton, CA 94588-8618
(800) 380-SOFT
peoplesoft.com
CRM/SFA software

Point Information Systems
65 William Street, Suite 150
Wellesley, MA 02481
(781) 416-7900
pointinfo.com
CRM sales, marketing, and service solutions

Salesforce.com
The Landmark at One Market, Suite 300
San Francisco, CA 94105
(415) 901-7000
salesforce.com
Hosted Web-based integrated CRM applications for sales force
    automation, customer service and support, and marketing
    automation

SalesLogix/ACT
8800 North Gainey Center Drive, Suite 200
Scottsdale, AZ 85258
(480) 368-3700
saleslogix.com
Customer relationship management solutions; small to mid-sized
    businesses

Salesnet
580 Harrison Avenue, Second Floor
Boston, MA 02118
(877) 350-0160
salesnet.com
Hosted Web-based sales force automation service

SAP
3999 West Chester Pike
Newtown Square, PA 19073
(610) 661-1000
sap.com
E-business platforms designed to help companies collaborate

Saratoga Systems
900 East Hamilton Avenue
Campbell, CA 95008
(877) 272-7286
saratogasystems.com/crm
Sales, marketing, and customer service management

Siebel
2207 Bridgepointe Parkway
San Mateo, CA 94404
(800) 647-4300
siebel.com
CRM/SFA software

Update.com Software
900 East Hamilton Avenue, Suite 100
Campbell, CA 95008
(408) 879-7472
update.com
Customer relationship management software

UpShot
1161 San Antonio Road
Mountain View, CA 94043
(650) 623-2200
upshot.com
Hosted Web-based CRM sales solution

Webcasting/Web Conferencing

Centra Software
430 Bedford Street, Second Floor
Lexington, MA 02420
(800) 414-3591
centra.com
E-meeting and conferencing

Genesys Conferencing
2001 Junipero Serra Boulevard
Daly City, CA 94014
(877) 263-6135
genesys.com
Web-based video conferencing

Placeware (recently purchased by Microsoft)
295 Bernardo Avenue
Mountain View, CA 94043
(888) 526-6170
placeware.com
Audio conferencing, presentation integration

Realnetworks
2601 Elliott Avenue, Suite 1000
Seattle, WA 98121
realnetworks.com/info/enterprise
(800) 444-8011
Desktop manager to customize employees' players and authorizing tool
    for creating educational and survey-based content

WebEx Communications
307 West Tasman Drive
San Jose, CA 95134
(877) 509-3239
webex.com
Application, presentation sharing, live video conferencing, recording,
    editing, playback, shared folder, and online scheduling

Yahoo!
701 First Avenue
Sunnyvale, CA 94089
(866) 267-7946
business.broadcast.com/webcast
Schedule, create, and manage live and pre-recorded video webcasts

Telemarketing Firms

Access Direct Telemarketing
4515 20th Avenue Southwest, Suite B
Cedar Rapids, IA 52404
(319) 390-8900
accdir.com
Outbound business-to-business

ASK Telemarketing
5815 Carmichael
Montgomery, AL 36117
(334) 387-2758
asktelemarketing.com
B2B expertise includes customer acquisition and retention, customer
    care, data modeling, customer management, and lead generation

Businesslink
4313 Fleur Drive
Des Moines, IA 50321
(800) 434-3221
marketlink.com
Specializes in market research, database enhancement, lead generation,
    lead qualification, and customer care

Lead Dogs
One Tech Plaza
2113 Wells Branch Parkway, Suite 4400
Austin, TX 78728
(800) 336-2616
leaddogs.com

Builds qualified prospect databases, manages and tracks direct
    marketing programs, specializes in advanced technologies

LiveBridge
7303 Southeast Lake Road
Portland, OR 97267
(503) 652-6000
livebridge.com
Provides technological support; helps develop a customer base and
    marketing strategies

MarketMakers Group
687 West Lancaster Avenue
Wayne, PA 19087
(610) 254-8924
marketmakersgroup.com
Designs customized teleservices programs

SoundBite
3 Burlington Woods
Burlington, MA 01803
(781) 273-3360
Interactive voice technology

Computer Service Bureaus/Data Enhancement

Anchor Computer
1900 New Highway
Farmingdale, NY 11735
(800) 966-9875
anchorcomputer.com
Data integrity, online and offline data standardization, and data
    matching or enhancing; real-time and batch address cleansing

Creative Automation
220 Fence Lane
Hillside, IL 60162

(800) 773-1588
cauto.com
Address deliverability, merge/purge, data enhancement, database
management, lifestyle and demographics

DataFlux
4001 Weston Parkway, Suite 300
Cary, NC 27513
(919) 674-2153
dataflux.com
Data correction and standardization, de-dupe, merge, and verification
online and offline

Dun & Bradstreet
103 JFK Parkway
Short Hills, NJ 07078
(973) 605-6288
dnb.com
Enhanced data services, global batch and data integration toolkit

Experian
475 Anton Boulevard
Costa Mesa, CA 92626
(888) 550-1182
experian.com
Data hygiene and verification, NCOA

Firstlogic
100 Harborview Plaza
La Crosse, WI 54601
(608) 782-5000
firstlogic.com
Data cleansing software and standardization

Group 1 Software
Maryland Office
4200 Parliament Place, Suite 600
Lanham, MD 20706-1844

(800) 368-5806
g1.com
Data hygiene and verification services

InfoUSA
5711 South 86th Circle
Omaha, NE 68127
(203) 552-6305
infousa.com
Data enhancement services; appending

Knowledgebase Marketing
701 North Plano Road
Richardson, TX 75081
(866) 456-9534
knowledgebasemarketing.com
Data hygiene and verification services

Market Models
85 Brown Street
Wickford, RI 02852
(800) 978-9508
marketmodels.com
Data enhancement services; appending

Melissa Data
22382 Avenida Empresa
Rancho Santa Margarita, CA 92688-2112
(949) 589-5200
melissadata.com
Batch verification and correction, enhancement of address and phone
    data

MeritDirect
333 Westchester Avenue
White Plains, NY 10468
(914) 368-1000
Profiling, segmentation, merge/purge

Merkle Direct Marketing
8400 Corporate Drive
Lanham, MD 20785
(301) 459-9700
merklenet.com
Address hygiene and standardization

Ruf Strategic Solutions
1533 East Spruce Street
Olathe, KS 66061
(800) 829-8544
ruf.com

Trillium Software (a division of Harte-Hanks)
25 Linnell Circle
Billerica, MA 01821
(978) 436-3332
trilliumsoft.com
Address hygiene and standardization

YellowBrick Solutions
2701 Aerial Center Parkway
Morrisville, NC 27713
(919) 653-2300
yellowbricksolutions.com
Address hygiene and standardization

Top B2B List Sources

Abacus
11101 West 120th Avenue
Broomfield, CO 80021
(303) 410-5100
abacusdirect.com

Advanstar Marketing Services
545 Boylston Street
Boston, MA 02116
(800) 225-4569
advanstarlists.com

American List Council
4300 Route 1
CN 5219
Preton, NJ 08543
(609) 580-2800
alc.com

B2Bworks
230 West Superior Street
Chicago, IL 60610
(888) 805-1595
b2bworks.net

Direct Media
200 Pemberwick Road
Greenwich, CT 06831
(203) 532-1000
directmedia.com

DM2 (formerly Cahners Business Lists)
2000 Clearwater Drive
Oak Brook, IL 60523
(800) 323-4958
cahnerslists.com

Dun & Bradstreet
103 JFK Parkway
Short Hills, NJ 07078
(973) 605-6288
dnb.com

Dunhill International List Co.
1951 Northwest 19th Street, Suite 200
Boca Raton, FL 33431
(561) 347-0200
dunhills.com

Edith Roman Associates
One Blue Hill Plaza, Suite 16
Pearl River, NY 10965
(800) 223-2194
edithroman.com

Experian
475 Anton Boulevard
Costa Mesa, CA 92626
(888) 550-1182
experian.com

Harris InfoSource
2057 East Aurora Road
Twinsburgh, OH 44087
(800) 888-5900

Hoover's Inc.
5800 Airport Boulevard
Austin, TX 78752
(512) 374-4500
hoovers.com

Hugo Dunhill Mailing Lists
30 East 33rd Street, 12th Floor
New York, NY 10016
(800) 223-6454
hdml.com

IDG List Services
500 Old Connecticut Path
Framingham, MA 01701
(888) 434-5478
idglist.com

InfoUSA
5711 South 86th Circle
Omaha, NE 68127
(203) 552-6305
infousa.com

Kroll Direct Marketing
101 Morgan Lane, Suite 120
Plainsboro, NJ 08536
(609) 275-2900
krolldirect.com

Lake Group Media
411 Theodore Fremd Avenue
Rye, NY 10580
(914) 925-2400
lakegrp.com

Leon Henry
455 Central Park Avenue
Scarsdale, NY 10583
(914) 723-3176
leonhenry.com

List Services Corp.
Six Trowbridge Drive
Bethel, CT 06801
(203) 743-2600
listservices.com

Mal Dunn Associates
2022 Route 22
Brewster, NY 10509
(914) 277-5558
maldunn.com

Merit Direct
333 Westchester Ave.
White Plains, NY 10468
(914) 368-1000
meritdirect.com

Penton Lists
1300 East Ninth Street
Cleveland, OH 44114
(216) 696-7000
pentonlists.com

Primedia Business Direct
11 Lake Avenue Extension
Danbury, CT 06811
(866) 226-4018
primediabusinessdirect.com

Response Media Products
3155 Medlock Bridge Road
Norcross, GA 30071
(770) 451-5478
responsemedia.com

Rubin Response Management Services
1111 North Plaza Drive, Suite 800
Schaumburg, IL 60173
(847) 619-9800
rubinresponse.com

24/7 Real Media
1250 Broadway, 28th Floor
New York, NY 10001
(800) 236-5790
247media.com

Venture Direct WorldWide
60 Madison Avenue, Floors 3 and 4
New York, NY 10010
(212) 684-4800
venturedirect.com

Walter Karl
One Blue Hill Plaza
Pearl River, NY 10965
(845) 620-0700
walterkarl.com

Worldata
3000 North Military Trail
Boca Raton, FL 33431
(800) 331-8102
worldata.com

Index